"Jim Canfield and I think alike. We believe that leadership is something you do *with* people, not something you do *to* people. Hire good people and treat them well. Work with them to set the vision and direction so they know where the organization is going. Listen to them and give them feedback—praise and redirection as needed—so they stay on track. Let them bring their brains to work so they feel involved and valued. And always celebrate victories together. It's not rocket science—it's just common sense. Read *CEO Tools 2.0* and get the tools you need to build a better future for yourself, your people, and your organization."

—**Ken Blanchard**, co-author of
The New One Minute Manager®;
co-editor of *Servant Leadership in Action*

"Culture is the No. 1 priority at Zappos. We know when we get that right, providing great customer service and building an enduring brand will fall into place. The tools featured in *CEO Tools 2.0* offer a guide to measure metrics, assess performance, and create a culture of ongoing improvement."

—**Tony Hsieh**, CEO, Zappos.com, Inc.; and *New
York Times* best-selling author of *Delivering Happiness*

"Although we're not related, Jim Canfield and I certainly share similar thoughts and ideas about what it takes to build a successful business. In *CEO Tools 2.0*, Jim outlines a system and provides the tools for any CEO, owner, or manager to create breakthrough results. Using the tools in this book is the path to transforming your business today."

—**Jack Canfield**, co-author of the best-selling
Chicken Soup for the Soul® series and *Success Principles™*

"When I worked with Jim Canfield, I knew him to be committed to helping leaders perform better. *CEO Tools 2.0* offers a solid platform with methods, tools, and techniques that any CEO or manager can use to improve results."

—**Ken Hamlet**, CEO, Monalex Partners;
former chairman, TEC Worldwide;
and former CEO, Holiday Inns, Inc.

"An accomplished CEO and CEO coach, Jim Canfield has assembled a treasure trove of tools and ideas to help other CEOs and business leaders take their companies and teams to the next level. This book is a great resource. Read it and grow!"

—**Wayne Cooper**, executive chairman, Chief Executive Group; publisher, CHIEF EXECUTIVE magazine; and CEO, Chief Executive Network

"One of the most important jobs of any leader is to put in place a sustainable business system that creates positive results. This book provides that step-by-step system, focusing on making it clear, making it happen, and making it better. When you read it, your challenge will be to pick the tools you want to implement that very day. This book is a goldmine."

—**Susan Scott**, CEO, Fierce, Inc.; author of *Fierce Conversations: Achieving Success at Work & in Life—One Conversation at a Time* and *Fierce Leadership: A Bold Alternative to the Worst "Best" Practices of Business Today*

"Tools belong in a toolbox, and Jim Canfield's classic book redux has created a new classic toolbox overflowing with practical, actionable advice for any smart exec or entrepreneur who wants to outpace the competition. Makers, mavericks, mavens, and mentors will make magic if they apply the principles in this masterpiece."

—**Chip Conley**, founder and former CEO, JDV Hotels; and *New York Times* best-selling author of *Peak: How Great Companies Get Their Mojo from Maslow*

"Most CEOs don't lack the will to become better. Rather, they lack a way that is doable by them given how little mind space they have to try anything beyond what they're already doing. *CEO Tools 2.0* is that way for them to take great strides in becoming better, more effective leaders with as little brain damage as possible."

—**Mark Goulston**, author of *Just Listen*, the world's top book on listening

"Strategic thinking is one of the most difficult leadership traits for a leader to understand. Jim Canfield's book will help you accelerate this process."

—**Jack Stack**, CEO, SRC Holdings Corp.;
and author of *The Great Game of Business*

"Jim Canfield has updated a classic, must-read primer for every entrepreneur or business leader. Read this book—and learn the tools to become an even better leader who creates an environment based on trust and gets better results."

—**Ruby Randall**, CEO, Tuesday LLC, Management Consulting;
former president and COO, Vistage International;
former president and CEO, Anthony Robbins Companies

"Jim Canfield's *CEO Tools 2.0* is a must-read for anyone in business. The book helps you take a look at yourself and the issues you are facing in your company in a way that makes everything crystal clear. Throughout the book, Jim used commonly faced problems and issues that every reader could relate to. The tools outlined are essential to running a company and improving results. I wish I had been given this book twenty years ago!"

—**Jania Bailey**, CFE and CEO, FranNet

"Jim Canfield has done the business world a great service by taking what Kraig Kramers started and creating the new book *CEO Tools 2.0*. This book gives executives and managers everything they need to form and run a high-performing business engine. I highly recommend this book."

—**Marshall Goldsmith**, world's No. 1 leadership
thinker; executive coach; and *New York Times*
best-selling author of *Triggers* and
What Got You Here, Won't Get You There

"Successful leaders never take their achievements for granted. They thirst for continuous self-improvement and understand how critically important it is to set and obtain the highest standards in their industry to secure the future of the enterprise and benefit the stakeholders, customers, employees, and communities they serve.

CEO Tools 2.0 is a wonderful guide to keep you on the right track and soar to new heights by utilizing basic DNA building blocks to keep your organization on the leading edge."

—**Debbi Fields**, founder and spokesperson,
Mrs. Field's Cookies and Bakeries;
and chairman, Debbi Fields Enterprises

"You can't make people do what's right. You can lead them, and you can empower them to make the right decisions. And if you want to create a culture that helps people win, *CEO Tools 2.0* provides the systems and tools to help build that culture in your company."

—**Garry Ridge**, president and CEO,
WD-40 Company; and co-author of
Helping People Win at Work

"*CEO Tools 2.0* is a rare gem in business publishing because it provides a tangible blueprint and exact stepping stones on how entrepreneurs can build fast-growth companies that last longer than cycles, fads, or trends. Good stuff from start to end."

—**Cliff Oxford**, CEO, Oxford Center for Entrepreneurs;
columnist, Forbes.com; and founder and former
CEO, STI Knowledge, Inc.

CEO TOOLS 2.0

CEO TOOLS 2.0

A System to *Think*, *Manage*, and *Lead* Like a CEO

JIM CANFIELD
and
KRAIG KRAMERS

Stonebrook Publishing
Saint Louis, Missouri

A STONEBROOK PUBLISHING BOOK

Copyright © Aprio CEO Tools IP, LLC
All rights reserved.

Edited by Nancy Erickson, The Book Professor
TheBookProfessor.com

Published in the United States by Stonebrook Publishing, a division of
Stonebrook Enterprises, LLC, Saint Louis, Missouri. No part of this book
may be reproduced, scanned, or distributed in any printed or electronic
form without written permission from the author.

Please do not participate in or encourage piracy of copyrighted
materials in violation of the author's rights.

Library of Congress Control Number: 2017960992

ISBN: 978-0-9975210-7-8

www.stonebrookpublishing.net

PRINTED IN THE UNITED STATES OF AMERICA

10 9 8 7 6 5 4 3 2 1

Contents

Part II: EXECUTE

PART III: OPTIMIZE

Prologue

It was 4:00 a.m., and Jack wasn't going back to sleep. He'd been wide awake since 2 o'clock, and his mind was leaping from one problem to another. Business used to be easier, he thought. As an electronics manufacturer and supplier, he'd once felt that he was on top of the world. Now his days revolved around competitive pressures, cash-flow issues, and a collapsing, directionless team.

Jack laced up his running shoes, hoping an early-morning run would clear his mind. For too long, he'd promised his wife that he'd get back in shape. Closing the front door quietly behind him, he headed out to the small lake at the end of his neighborhood.

The run, more challenging than he remembered, was helping him wipe the problems from his thoughts. It had been awhile since he'd taken on the hills around the lake.

As he crested the last hill at the end of his hour-long run, Jack's glance focused on a bench next to the water fountain. He couldn't wait to collapse on it, but a man who looked to be in his late sixties was sitting there.

"Whoa, there!" the man said, adjusting his glasses and smiling at Jack. "What are you running from?"

"What makes you think I'm running from something?" Jack asked.

"Well, the way I see it, people are either running from something or running to something. You, my friend, look like a man who's running from something. Am I wrong about that?" he asked.

Jack coughed out a laugh and said, "Well, I guess not. But I don't actually think of it as running away. I'm trying to clear my head. I've got a lot of tough issues to deal with at my company right now."

"I understand," the man said, "and probably better than you could know. I've run a few companies myself, and it's not easy. What's going on, if I might ask?"

Jack wasn't sure he wanted to talk about his business concerns with a stranger. But perhaps talking would be therapeutic.

"It used to be so much easier to run the business," he confessed. "We were smaller back then and full of energy. Everyone seemed to know where we were headed, and we all did everything we could to make things happen. We had a great team: we relied on each other and watched each other's backs, making the most out of every little victory, no matter how small."

"What changed?" asked the stranger.

"As the business grew," Jack explained, "everyone splintered into different directions, trying to serve different customer needs. Now the manufacturing and distribution departments struggle to keep up with the promises the sales and marketing teams make to our customers, and they're always at odds with each other.

"And we're never sure if the changes we make to fix our problems are helping or hurting. In fact, sales have dropped, so cash flow is tight. Some of our people have been with us a long time, but they aren't qualified to take us to the next level. And then there's me. I don't think I'm as effective as a leader as I used to be—or as I need to be now."

Jack stopped short, thinking he might have revealed more to this man than he should have. After all, who was this guy anyway?

Preface

I'm not the guy on the bench, but I've had the good fortune to combine my own experience of starting, building, and running several businesses with what I've learned from twenty-five years of coaching hundreds of amazing and impressive business owners—who've struggled to create profitable, successful companies with highly aligned and engaged teams. These business owners have spanned a wide variety of industries, including manufacturing, distribution, services, and technology, and they've ranged from startups to highly profitable entrepreneurial firms to $400 million enterprises.

I spent over two decades leading CEO peer groups. Executive peer groups are more common today than when I led my first one in the mid-1990s, and they remain one of the greatest secret weapons for any business leader looking to improve and grow a company. An executive peer group allows participating CEOs, owners, and executives to discuss their most pressing issues with a dozen other like-minded group members—to address their challenges, get input from the other members, and create opportunities to grow.

During this time, I met some of the world's top thought leaders on business, success, and productivity. Their influence has become a major part of the philosophies I embrace on how to run a more effective business while living a more rewarding life. And that's how I met Kraig Kramers.

Kraig was a force of nature—a man who seemed to have unlimited amounts of energy and drive. Of the more than 300 speakers we booked, only a few presented ideas and concepts that our CEOs adopted and used for years down the line—because they produced great results. Kraig Kramers was one of those people.

When I met Kraig, he'd been CEO of seven companies in seven industries. In most cases, he'd been hired to turn the companies around. His expertise was moving a company that was struggling, floundering, or flat-out failing to a place of growth and profitability. In each of these companies, he succeeded in an incredibly short amount of time—and he did it by using the tools and techniques in this book, which Kraig first presented in his 2002 book titled *CEO Tools: The Nuts-n-Bolts of Business for Every Manager's Success.*

Sadly, Kraig Kramers died in 2014, at the age of seventy-two. But the ideas and concepts that fueled Kraig's successes and the successes of many other business leaders are simply too important to be forgotten. They are alive and vibrant today in this updated and expanded version of his original book: *CEO Tools 2.0.*

Don't be fooled by the title of this new version. It's not just for CEOs but rather for any CEO, executive, owner, or manager who needs and wants to get better results. In fact, the acronym *CEO* isn't used in this book as a short version of chief executive officer. As you'll learn in the introduction, I've used the letters C, E, and O to stand for, respectively, Communicate, Execute, and Optimize.

The information you'll find within these pages can transform your business—and your life—if you choose to implement these tools. You don't have to attack them all at once. Just pick one and get started. The best time to begin is now.

Introduction

I've asked hundreds of CEOs, presidents, business owners, and senior executives who have come to me for help with their companies the same question: "How would you like your company to change?" Three answers surfaced most often. The first answer was *increased growth and profits*. These leaders said they wanted to generate growing revenues with improved profit margins and more predictable, reliable cash flow.

The second most frequent response was *easier execution*. This group wanted to be sure that everyone on their team was on the same page and working together to accomplish the organization's strategic plans and objectives. And these leaders wanted this to happen without their direct involvement in day-to-day operations.

The third thing they wanted was *more time*. They wanted the company to achieve better profits and growing revenues without their direct involvement, so they could have more time—more time with their families, more time to travel, and more time for their hobbies and other interests.

But the odds are generally stacked against business leaders who want to achieve these goals. Only one business in ten will have revenue that exceeds $1 million and more than ten employees. Only one in one hundred businesses will grow revenues above $10 million with more than twenty-five employees. And if you want to break through to build a $100 million business, the odds are one in 1,000.

How can you beat those odds? If more profit from your growing business is the *what*, and more time for yourself is the *why*, this book's tools, techniques, and templates will show you *how*. For our purposes, *tools* refer to anything that helps you get a job done easier, faster, or more effectively. Tools can be methods, programs, techniques, or assessments; and tools can refer to an action, process, or worksheet.

Chances are, you're not in business all by yourself: you have employees. And most employees need the answers to three questions to be effective:

- Where are we headed?

- How am I doing?

- What can I do to make things better?

To help you provide your employees with the answers to these three questions, this book is divided into three parts: Part I: **C**ommunicate; Part II: **E**xecute; and Part III: **O**ptimize.

In Part I, you'll find tools and techniques to *make it clear* where the company is headed. In Part II are tools designed to *make it happen*, so your employees understand how they're doing. And the tools in Part III will show you how to *make it better*. At the end of each chapter is a case study of a company that has applied the practices, methods, and tools consistent with what you will find in this book.

There's also an opportunity for you to create a giant leap in your business that goes beyond both the tools and the process. At this level, everything goes right; everything moves in synchronized harmony. When you're ready to conduct your business like a finely tuned orchestra, this is the path. It's getting to the state of *WE*.

Achieving the Power of *WE*

You're holding a complete tool chest of tested, on-point management tools that can help you make more money, catalyze customer service, enhance employee satisfaction, and make it more fun to be in business. Implemented together, they can carry your organization from *us* and *them* through the power of *WE*.

To realize ongoing, superlative results, you must have a solid, well-practiced business system that transforms your business to the magic of *WE*. In this state, all stakeholders in the business—employees, customers, suppliers, and the community—are totally aligned to the direction, goals, and methods and are willing to take action that creates results.

Hollow team-building that's disconnected from a consistent business system and appropriate organizational development won't get you to *WE*. By contrast, consistently applying the right tools and walking the talk in each critical area *will* get you there.

Actually, there's a short cut to get to a culture of *WE* rather quickly. It involves embedding a systematic business system that uses communication and recognition tools. It won't occur overnight, but you'll score some successes here and a few more there. And then one day—as you're walking the four corners of your business—you'll discover that the *WE* synergy exists in your company. You'll *see* it, and you'll *feel* it.

It likely will be hard to pinpoint the exact moment of the transformation. But you'll know when it has occurred because it's like a locomotive under full steam; it's rolling, and you can't stop it.

The Spirit and Language of *WE*

Employees will be happy doing their jobs and making things happen in the company. You'll no longer hear about the us-versus-them tension or that's-not-my-job sentiments that are all too common these days. Instead, you'll hear, "Wow, we sure helped Jane Customer today!" and "Tough day, but we got it done!" Or you'll hear, "Production is a little behind, but not to worry. We'll get there."

Achieving the *WE* culture takes hard work, dedication, and consistent application of a business system—plus a commitment to continual learning. Once you're there, your organization can accomplish anything it sets out to achieve, and no competitor will be able touch you.

The companies featured in the case studies that follow each chapter of this book are from different industries and vary in size, but they all clearly exhibit and are strengthened by the power of *WE*. Let these companies—all world-class businesses—be the inspiration for your own company's journey to harness the power of *WE*.

The CEO Tools Business System

What's your business system? What tools do you as a leader or manager use to get results? Are your tools consistent? Do your tools produce reliable results? What's the sequence for using those tools?

Don't be surprised or shocked if you can't answer these questions. Even successful chief executives and other leaders can't always pinpoint what creates their results—whether positive or negative. But that doesn't have to be you. You can learn the CEO Tools Business System, a singular, step-by-step business system that uses specific tools to produce results. These steps and tools are repeatable, and they produce consistent results.

Using this business system requires patience and a willingness to change. In many cases, you'll be encouraged to do things not only *differently* than you have in the past but in direct *opposition* to your past practices. You'll learn how to take a closer look at what you do to achieve your business goals and then take action to improve your methods and processes.

The CEO Tools Business System

COMMUNICATE • **E**XECUTE • **O**PTIMIZE

There's a chapter in this book that addresses each of the seven steps of the CEO Tools Business System:

- **Step 1: Set the Direction**—Clarify your overall goals, vision, and action plans using a *One-Page Business Plan.* Make it clear by distributing copies to all employees to share and communicate to your business targets. Translate the plans for all employees to help everyone focus on what is most important. Set big, audacious goals (BAGs) together. Big results happen by reaching higher than expected.

- **Step 2: Communicate to Build Trust**—Start by listening to every employee at every level of your business. The best tool here is *Walk the Four Corners* (W4C) of your business. Ask people how to improve the company, how to fix problems, and how to seize opportunities. If you ask often and listen hard, they'll shower you with solutions.

- **Step 3: Track Metrics and Give Feedback**—Break your long-term goals into workable chunks with the *Quarterly Priorities Manager (QPM)*. The QPM may be the single most powerful management tool for any business. Another metric-driven tool is the *Trailing 12-Month Chart (T12M)*, the most meaningful measurement tool in business. It's a rolling annual total chart that instantly reflects every key performance indicator.

- **Step 4: Anticipate the Future and Create It**—Using *What's Next?* to anticipate changes in your business or industry can allow you to capitalize when others falter. Build the seven key plans that every business should have in place to ensure the company's future and your own.

- **Step 5: Attract, Hire, and Coach Winners**—Look inside your company to determine the three to five key customer-impacting jobs. These jobs have the potential to make the biggest impact on customers—either positive or negative. Put winners in those jobs and be sure they agree on what constitutes excellent performance. Then give them the tools, training, compensation, and recognition to produce that level of performance.

- **Step 6: Build an Autonomous Company**—Build a business that can run without your day-to-day involvement. Create a company where senior leaders focus on the long-term strategic issues and are confident that daily operations are on track.

- **Step 7: Celebrate Successes**—Recognition and appreciation are the secret engine that drives ongoing success and accomplishment. Spread recognition and appreciation throughout the company by creating a peer recognition program that provides a fun way for employees at all levels to recognize each other for outstanding job performance and to appreciate other team members' contributions.

The overview above touches on only some of the tools that are discussed in this book. Each tool can guide you to make your business better *right now*. Of course, you'll want to adapt the tools to your own style, so plan to fine-tune them to fit the way you do things. Encourage others in your organization to do the same, within appropriate guidelines that you set.

This business system and the tools within it have a distinct order. When you follow the process from start to finish and apply the tools in succession, you'll see the greatest results. But if you're desperate for a quick fix for a current issue in need of a jump start or a turnaround, you can use the overview to guide you to the chapter that might provide the tools you need to tackle for that particular challenge.

The goal of this book is to make it easy to implement the right tools in every business area and for every business function. The best news for you may be that you don't have to be the one to implement every tool. You can share this book and its concepts with your key players and help them implement the tools that fit the organization. By doing this, you'll almost certainly cover all the business areas that need attention, areas that you may have neglected or even avoided in the past.

Part I
COMMUNICATE

Chapter One
Set the Direction

The CEO Tools Business System

COMMUNICATE • EXECUTE • OPTIMIZE

> If you don't know where you are going,
> then any road will get you there.
>
> —Lewis Carroll, *Alice in Wonderland*

"You have fractured teams, an undefined market, some incompetent employees, and cash-flow issues," the stranger said. "That's a lot to have on your mind. Can I ask you a question or two?"

Jack figured it couldn't hurt, and it was still early anyway. So he replied, "Sure. Go ahead."

The man spoke in a brisk, staccato style with the energy of a much younger man. "There's a part in Alice in Wonderland, when Alice asks the Cheshire Cat which way she should go. The cat, in turn, asks where she's headed. When Alice responds that she doesn't really know, he says, 'If you don't know where you are going, then any road will get you there.' So, my friend, do you know where you're going?"

The question rocked Jack. He stammered for a moment and then said, "I'm not really sure. We clearly have a mix of problems."

"Like what?" the stranger asked.

"To start with, I think we've been trying to serve too many markets. Some are declining and will never come back.

"And we've got employee issues. We're afraid of losing them, so we don't give them the feedback they need to do their jobs well. And some of our employees who used to perform well don't fit current roles; we haven't done anything about that.

"Our data gives us information without any real insights. But I don't have to look at data to know we've lost the sense of camaraderie and the energy we once had."

"Sounds a lot like what I faced when I was the chief executive of a printing company," the stranger shared.

"You had the same problems?" Jack asked.

"Not problems. Challenges. Problems are what people talk about instead of doing something. Challenges are obstacles that winners overcome on their paths to victory," he clarified.

"What did you do when you faced these . . . challenges?" Jack inquired.

"I'd be happy to tell you, but do you have time?"

Jack glanced at his watch. 5:15 a.m. It would be at least a couple of hours before anyone showed up at work. He nodded for the stranger to continue.

"The first step is to set the direction. Nothing is worse than telling people to work harder when what they're doing doesn't produce results.

It's demoralizing, and it erodes their trust. They know it's not working, and so do you.

"Make the direction clear for them. Tell them where you're going. Give them something simple they can see and pursue."

Jack nodded. "How did you make it clear for your employees?"

The man pulled out a small notebook and wrote down some notes for Jack to take back to the office.

The Leader Sets Direction

As the leader, it's your responsibility to set the direction for the organization. You're also responsible for communicating the company's goals throughout the organization in *clear* and *meaningful* terms. *Clear* means the goals are easy to understand; *meaningful* means the goals are significant and relevant.

● ● ●

The goal at Graphic Arts Center (GAC), a major commercial printing company that was based in Portland, Oregon, was to double annual sheet-fed printing sales—which represented about 20 percent of revenue—from $12 million to $24 million over the next two years. This targeted rate of growth for a two-year period was extremely aggressive: six times the industry growth rate. If GAC doubled sheet-fed sales and production over two years, it would realize compounded growth of over 40 percent per year.

All seven regional sales managers said they could do it and wanted to try. They knew it would be personally challenging, which made it fun. The company had grown at a similar rate in the past; and even though the numbers were smaller back then, it would be exciting to take on this new challenge and work to make it happen.

For the company to be successful, all GAC stakeholders had to understand the direction and believe that it was meaningful—employees and managers, of course, as well as customers, suppliers, and the community.

How did GAC make its direction clear and meaningful? The message was literally everywhere. Signs posted on the walls clarified the direction, and it was discussed at every meeting at every level of the company. Managers reiterated the direction as they walked the four corners of the business, and even customers and suppliers got to know the familiar chorus.

A goal is like a dartboard. You don't have to hit the bull's-eye every time to score; you can earn points simply by getting on the board. Your company goals must be so clear and so meaningful that they move every constituency toward the bull's-eye. When the goals are meaningful motivators, *everyone* will want to play, and *everyone* will get a shot at the board.

What made the goal of doubling sheet-fed volume meaningful enough to get all of GAC's stakeholders excited? If the company reached the goal, it would have enough profit to buy new sheet-fed printing presses and grow its labor force, which motivated every company constituency. Customers would benefit because new, state-of-the-art presses would produce the highest-quality printed products. Employees were energized because the goal communicated that the company was willing to invest in modernization; the new, state-of-the-art presses would give them bragging rights in the industry. And increased business might mean pay raises and even bonuses. Suppliers were behind the initiative because higher GAC production volumes meant higher purchases of paper and ink. Finally, the community got on board because increased revenue translated to more jobs, and the new, more efficient machinery would reduce emissions beyond what was required.

GAC communicated its message with clarity and meaning to each of these groups, helping it toward its ambitious goal.

Define the Direction

The direction—again, which is *your* job to set for your company—is represented by this pyramid:

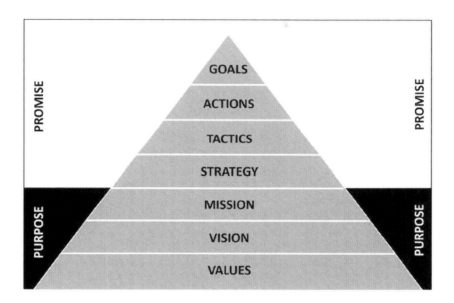

The three planks at the base of the pyramid represent the *aspirational purpose* of your organization—what the company could be at peak performance.

- **Values**—Your values clarify who the company is and how it acts. Values, once identified, must be defined. People often choose words like *integrity*, which seem self-explanatory; but it's important to specifically define what it means to act with integrity at *your* company. Your values define the company culture, and they state not only what's permitted, but also what won't be tolerated.

- **Vision**—Your vision portrays the ultimate version of what the company will become if things go according to plan.

- **Mission**—Your mission is what you do, how you do it, who you serve, and what results you deliver.

The next four planks represent the organization's *inspirational promise*. A promise equals a commitment—a commitment to action and to results. The promise motivates your employees to action so they can achieve the desired outcomes.

- **Strategy**—Your strategy is what the company will accomplish over the next two to three years to embody its defined mission, vision, and values.

- **Tactics**—Your tactics list how your strategies will be accomplished this year.

- **Actions and goals**—Your actions are the short-term actions you'll take in the coming months or quarters to reach the goals you plan to achieve.

Establish and Communicate Clear Goals

Nothing leads to success like having clear, written goals that are continually communicated to every constituency. Unfortunately, most companies' goals are largely unknown outside senior management, and senior managers often may have only a vague understanding of the goals. To get where you want to go, everyone from the person who sweeps the floors at night to the chief executive must know where the company is headed, what the company goals are, why the goals are important, and what their specific role is in achieving the goals.

Six principles for setting and then pursuing goals can have a tremendous impact on the performance of both individuals and the organization as a whole:

- **Bring the team together to set goals**—Never set goals for others without their involvement. People will work harder to achieve the goals they create themselves, especially when working in a group. Let your people set the goals. And be sure that they are measurable.

- **Create the budget**—Your budget reflects the minimum acceptable performance for your company or group, and it serves as the baseline for your goals. The budget figures aren't negotiable; they're do-or-die targets for sales, costs, and expenses. Your budget should be realistic and achievable, but also somewhat challenging so that the goals reflect an outcome you'd be happy to accomplish.

- **Set bigger, more audacious goals**—Next, set some bigger, more audacious goals that are a stretch to reach. The big, audacious goal is the bull's-eye of a dartboard; everyone still gets points if they miss the center but land on the board. Position these so it's fun to shoot for them and a big win even if you fall short. Include a compensation structure with accelerators that kick in if your employees perform above budget.

- **Test the goals**—Test the goals against the company values and check for alignment with all parts of your business strategy. Are they in sync? If not, make the necessary changes.

- **Communicate the goals**—Communicate the goals over and over again. Then communicate them some more. (Some tools to aid communication are in the next chapter.)

- **Provide rewards and feedback**—Praise and reward all behaviors and any results that support reaching the goals. Provide ongoing, positive feedback to show your employees that it's important to achieve the goals and to prime them for the next round of goal achievement.

Help Employees Write Goals

To help your employees write clear, measurable goals, here's a formula, followed by an example. The formula and example make it easy to teach others to set effective goals.

Goal Setting 101

VERB + NOUN + OUT-COME + DATE = GOAL

Example: Increase (verb) sales (noun) from $60 million to
$100 million (outcome) by December 31, 2019 (date).

Set Big, Audacious Goals

Setting big, audacious goals can help you and your employees achieve results beyond your wildest dreams. Big, audacious goals (BAGs) are about what's *possible*, not *probable*. (In his quintessential leadership book, *Good to Great*, Jim Collins used a similar phrase: Big Hairy Audacious Goals, or BHAGs.)

Too often, we get stuck in the status quo of what's probable. But if you want your people to accomplish really amazing things, try setting BAGs with them.

How fast can you ride a bike? Speeds of 10, 15, or maybe 20 miles an hour probably come to mind. However, what if the question were asked a different way: What is the fastest someone could ride a bike? Now, you might say 25, 30, or even 40 miles an hour. But what if you found out that someone once rode a bicycle at a speed of 151 miles an hour?

John Howard rode a bicycle at 151.85 miles per hour in 1985, becoming the fastest person ever on a bicycle; Howard's amazing record remains to this day. Granted, he had a special bicycle, was riding on the Bonneville Salt Flats, and was drafting a specially designed vehicle with full aerodynamic features to shelter him from the buffeting wind. Nonetheless, one man on two wheels under human power rode a bicycle at almost 152 miles an hour.

That's the difference between what is *probable* and what is *possible*. Big Audacious Goals are about what's possible. If you really want your people to accomplish amazing things, try setting big, audacious goals with them.

The best big, audacious goals are acceptable challenges; for example, showing a profit in a month that has consistently registered a loss. But a BAG doesn't have to be stated in terms of total revenue or dollars. A BAG can target the number of units sold, the number of happy customers, or the number of client cases resolved successfully. Or a BAG can be aspirational; for example, winning a Best Place to Work award or being named to *Inc.* magazine's *Inc.* 1,000 list. A BAG can be *any* measure of quality or customer satisfaction, or just about *anything* that can lead to outstanding performance for the organization as a whole.

No matter what you decide to target and measure, the secret to success is making sure everyone in the company understands the BAG, has fun going for it, and stays focused on it with laser-beam precision. This, again, means setting a very clear goal and then communicating it over and over and over again. Once you get the goal right, amazing things can happen.

● ● ●

The example of Graphic Arts Center (GAC) shows just how powerful a BAG can be. At GAC, sales had gone flat and stayed that way, despite slow but steady overall growth in the industry. When a company stalls out like that, many things can happen, and most of them aren't good. People get bored and frustrated because they no longer feel challenged or successful. Profits drop because expenses keep climbing, even when sales don't. The focus turns to expense-cutting, and investment in the company is minimal. The sense of fun and camaraderie gets replaced by cynicism and finger-pointing. Pretty soon, the winners leave. (Why is it that underperformers seldom leave on their own?) The company drops into complacency, followed by a slow decline.

A question was posed in a meeting with the seven GAC regional sales managers: "How do we get things going again?"

Startled, one sales manager asked, "You mean growth?"

Another observed, "Our last chief executive never talked about growth. He was stuck in the drone zone." This woman meant that the pace of the pack can't exceed the pace of the leader. Think about a dog-sled team as an example.

Finally, one sales manager ventured, "We know how to grow. It's with sheet-fed print jobs. Those orders produce twice the gross margin as web-press print jobs, which take three to nine months to print and bill. But sheet-fed orders get printed, shipped, and billed in just a few days."

That prompted the next question to the sales managers: "How fast can we grow sheet-fed?"

Another manager spoke up. "Our competitors average 4 percent to 8 percent growth per year for sheet-fed, but we can do much better than that. I think we can double our production in two years if we get aggressive. We've grown that fast before."

By articulating this BAG, the manager got everyone's attention. The tone of the room completely shifted, and excitement filled the air.

Then, as often happens, someone in the back of the room spoke up as a voice of reason.

"Hold on, folks. We need new sheet-fed printing presses. There's no way we can double production without them."

But they couldn't rush out to buy new presses. The company was barely profitable. And even if the company had the money, it didn't make sense to fill up a room with eight $1.5 million printing presses before business was at a level to justify the cost. Maybe there was a way to *earn* the new equipment.

The group developed a plan to grow sheet-fed business as fast as possible. After three or four months of being on track to meet the BAG, they'd get one new, state-of-the-art sheet-fed press. The team rallied around the idea of earn-it-as-you-go. It was both logical and a challenge—and people love challenges, as long as they're framed in a sensible, achievable way.

The company planned to acquire a new press every few months, as long as growth continued at the pace to meet their goal of doubling every two years. Everyone at GAC bought into the concept.

The best part was the fun they had chasing after that BAG. When a sheet-fed job order came in, someone would run down the hall shouting, "Sheet-fed, sheet-fed!" A chorus of applause and shouts then followed—not because anyone encouraged it, but because the BAG had created a camaraderie that in turn created a fun atmosphere.

Despite their best efforts, however, the company didn't quite double sheet-fed sales in two years. At the end of the second year, the company had realized $23.9 million in sales—99 percent of the BAG.

• • •

The moral of the story, of course, is that if GAC had set the goal at $18 million—a daunting target in and of itself—it would never have come anywhere near $23.9 million. Thanks to having set a BAG, the company came darned close to hitting $24 million, and the last two or three million dollars of sales volume were almost pure profit.

Although GAC failed to meet its BAG, the team celebrated their success, and in doing so, cemented an ongoing commitment to have fun with new, challenging goals. And celebrating made those big goals a regular way of life, as you'll read in chapter seven.

> Asked how he knew how to turn a failing company around, turnaround expert Jerry Goldress replied, "I ask the people working there. They always know what to do. They've just lost the will to do it."

Define Your Unique Sales Proposition

What does your company do that's better than everyone else? What differentiates you from your competitors? What's your "secret sauce"? More importantly, do your customers and suppliers clearly understand what you do so well, and would they attest to it?

This is your company's unique sales proposition (USP), defining your prime focus. Your USP gives your employees something to be proud of, is a key component of your value proposition, and is a benchmark for your suppliers.

To define your USP, ask:

- What is unique, different, unusual, or compelling about our company?

- What does our company do? What business are we actually in?

- How do our customers describe us?

- Why do customers come to us in the first place?

- Why do current customers come back for repeat business?

- Why do we lose customers to competitors?

As you'll see in the next section, the USP is a key driver of the One-Page Business Plan and the foundation for the vision of the company or team. Think of it this way: imagine the power of being able to articulate your company's fundamental value proposition in one or two sentences.

• • •

After much discussion, the GAC team realized that they weren't just selling high-end commercial printing. They were selling positive image—pieces that promoted their clients' products, ideas, and concepts. In fact, their customers had started calling it "GAC quality," and it had become the industry standard. It connoted more than quality; it reflected the value-added nuances that GAC added to the final design and delivery of the printed piece. GAC leveraged this distinction to differentiate how it promoted customers' products and services and its interactions and relationships with its customers.

Here's the unique sales proposition proposition that GAC ultimately created:

> *GAC is the leading fine-color commercial printer in the United States. We serve America's most dynamic businesses with top-quality printing of advertising literature, specialty catalogs, and annual reports.*

Fine-color was the generic replacement for *GAC quality,* and GAC was able to get the industry—meaning customers and competitors—to use the new term.

Create and Circulate a One-Page Business Plan

Our job as leaders is to get our team members to accomplish the goals of our company, division, or functional area. Few things are more demoralizing than devoting scarce resources, time, energy, and money to something and then discover you've been chasing the wrong objective.

The One-Page Business Plan is a simple, effective tool that will get your organization sharply focused on its direction and goals. It will help ensure that your people are moving in the right direction by clearly showing them what your company wants to do and how you'll do it.

As you can see below, there are three sections addressing the organization's vision; strategies and tactics; and metrics, goals, and responsibilities.

In the first column, you'll record your company's vision, mission, and values—the three planks at the base of the pyramid introduced earlier. The next two columns of the form provide a place to record your strategies to accomplish the mission and vision, as well as the tactics you'll employ to achieve the strategies. Five strategies are enough; any more will confuse and diffuse the efforts. Each of the five strategies can have up to five tactics for action.

The next three columns show what you'll measure for the various tactics, what the goals are for each outcome, and who's responsible to track and support each initiative. There's room to add a big, audacious goal and to highlight the most important customer-impacting jobs, which are explored in chapter five.

Let's walk through creating a single strategy for a One-Page Business Plan.

STRATEGY 2-3 years	TACTICS Annually		METRICS	GOALS	OWNER
What we will accomplish	How we will accomplish Strategy		What we will Measure	Target/Results	Who will track
Strategy 1	Tactics to Accomplish Strategy 1				
	1	Target prospects who have current customer profile with marketing and sales program	1 Conversion ratio - new prospects - new customers	30%	Darren
	2	Target prospects who are similar or adjacent to current customer profile with campaign	2 Conversion ratio - new prospects - new customers	30%	Darren
To increase revenues through acquisition of new accounts	3	Develop and implement compensation financing for new account acquisition	3 Number of new accts opened	125	Ryan
	4	Develop new acct pricing and financing structure	4 Revenue generated by new accounts	$125,000	Ryan
	5	Develop a testimonial and referral program for existing customers and referral sources	5 Conversion ratio - referrals - new customers	55%	Darren

In this example, the strategy is to increase revenues through acquisition of new accounts. There are five tactics to accomplish this strategy:

- Target prospects who match our current customer profile with a marketing and sales program.

- Target prospects who are similar to the current customer profile with marketing and sales campaigns.

- Develop and implement a compensation structure to reward the sales team for new account acquisition.

- Develop a new account pricing model and structure.

- Develop a testimonial and referral program for existing customers and other referral sources.

In the third column are the metrics to be used to measure progress, such as the ratio of converting new prospects to customers and the number of new accounts opened. Each metric has an associated goal in the fourth column signifying a successful outcome for the strategy and tactics and, in the fifth column, an individual responsible for monitoring progress and reporting on the status.

When you've fleshed out one strategy in this manner, do the same for your other strategies. The One-Page Business Plan that you create will be an at-a-glance snapshot of the tactics, metrics, goals, and responsible parties that you'll follow to move your company toward the direction you've established.

Now put your One-Page Business Plan in every employee's hands so they'll commit to moving the organization forward. And be sure to use this tool for frequent conversations with your team members about their individual actions that drive the desired outcomes more effectively.

Motivate Your People to Action

Setting ambitious goals and sharing them with the entire team is one thing; achieving them is another. Goals should be linked to aggressive compensation plans that reward your employees for achieving them. Interestingly, it's usually a company's current top performers who are motivated by challenging goals and aggressive compensation plans.

Money is the most commonly used motivator, but it's actually considered a *base motivator*. To get your superstars to reach for higher and higher levels, you must understand their personal dreams and find ways to help fulfill them. When you do, there's nothing you can't accomplish together.

Have you heard through the grapevine or in private discussions that an employee wants or needs something special but can't or won't buy it? Make that *something* his or her reward for hitting a big, auda-cious goal. It could be a trip to an exotic place, a Harley-Davidson® motorcycle, a one-year lease on an incredible sports car, or a hot tub on the back patio—anything that represents the employee's long-held desire.

At one company, Ken, the top regional sales manager, had added a big, beautiful music room to his home. But two years later, it still sat empty. Ken and his wife loved classical music and wanted a grand piano for the room. But something had kept the music room empty. Did writing a check for a $30,000 piano seem too much to the couple? Did buying a Steinway feel too showy?

At work, Ken was offered a two-tiered incentive plan. If his region achieved $5.5 million in sales with a profit of at least $795,000 in the upcoming quarter, the company would present him with a world-class Kawai grand piano valued at $11,000. But if Ken could produce a $915,000 profit, he'd be awarded a Steinway grand piano, the very same model that world-famous pianist Vladimir Horowitz owned—valued at over $32,000 at the time.

This type of plan is "the Grand Solution," playing on the piano Ken could acquire. This incentive plan really lit a fire under Ken—who now has a Steinway grand piano at home, installed by his company! It was an absolutely stunning finish to Ken's music room. And the look of pride and pleasure on Ken's face when that piano arrived far outweighed the impact of receiving a bonus check.

Setting a challenging goal is only half the equation. To keep your employees on track to achieve it, be sure to pepper them with lots of encouragement, enthusiastic support, and ongoing feedback. Ken's company encouraged him by sending him the latest Steinway catalog and awarding him a state-of-the-art metronome after his first successful month, and the company continued to offer Ken support and recognition at every opportunity.

If you use this type of incentive, there are three things to consider:

- **Be prepared**—Be prepared with a plan for what will happen if the employee gets close to the goal but falls short. In Ken's case, if he'd achieved only 90 percent of the target, he'd still have received the Steinway; but for every percentage point he fell short, he'd have had to write a check to the company for the difference.

- **Don't forget taxes**—Someone is obligated to pay taxes on the piano, which essentially was compensation to Ken. The best approach is to "gross up" the reward by writing a check to the employee for the taxes owed.

- **Follow through**—Be sure to deliver the reward in a timely manner. When people work hard to help achieve the company's goals, you must hold up your end of the bargain by delivering the reward without delay. The closer you link the reward to the employee's positive behavior, the easier it will be to influence his or her behavior the next time.

The important thing is to have *fun* with your challenges to your employees. They'll appreciate the creativity and will love the distraction from their normal quotas or performance expectations. They'll enjoy a friendly competition that rewards them with something that *they* truly want rather than something that *you* want to give them.

Top Tools to Set the Direction

- **One-Page Business Plan**—Create a one-page plan to define a common direction. Spell out your goals, purpose, and strategy. Include your unique sales proposition and big, audacious goals. Share it with everyone in the company and continually communicate the message.

- **Strategic alignment**—Develop five strategies that will move the company forward over the next two or three years. Next, generate five tactics for each strategy to accomplish this year. Then break it down into specific actions to be done each quarter to do what is needed now.

- **Accountability**—Include a metric to track and a goal to shoot for, and assign a specific person responsible for tracking the progress and requesting resources.

- **Big, audacious goals (BAGs)**—Have some fun by setting some really challenging BAGs within your overall goals. Make each BAG a real stretch that's attainable with superstar effort and coordination. Make it okay to fall short of a BAG as long as you achieve or exceed base budgets.

- **Reinforcement**—Use repetitive communication about goals and give everyone encouragement. Goals become a positive challenge rather than a meaningless chore.

- **Unique sales proposition**—Establish the reasons your customers buy from you and the ways your company and its products/services are unique in your industry.

- **The "Grand Solution"**—To achieve remarkable results, help make your employees' dreams come true. Make their dreams a reward for achieving a BAG and enthusiastically support the employee's effort.

- **Goal Setting 101**—Teach employees how to write a goal using this formula.

For Further Thought

- What do goals mean in your business?
- Are your goals clear? Do you communicate them to your people?
- Do your employees know where the company is headed, what it will take to get there, and how you'll win?
- Are your people focused on goals or obstacles?
- Is your team motivated deep down to achieve your goals, ready to hurdle every obstacle?
- How are you having fun with your goals?

CEO Tools Case Study:
Frieda's, Inc., Los Alamitos, California

When you think of innovation, new technologies or scientific breakthroughs may come to mind rather than produce. But without the vision and efforts of Frieda Rapoport Caplan, professional chefs and home cooks in the United States—and consumers—wouldn't have easy access to healthy foods such as kiwifruit, spaghetti squash, shiitake mushrooms, Belgian endive, passion fruit, or dragon fruit. In fact, if you've ever walked through the produce department at your local grocery and asked yourself, "What's that?" the mystery fruit or vegetable probably came through Frieda's.

Founded in 1962, Frieda's, Inc. is a third-generation, woman-owned family business that markets and distributes specialty produce. Frieda's two daughters now own and operate the company: CEO and President Karen Caplan and COO and Vice President Jackie Caplan Wiggins. Karen's daughter, Alex Jackson Berkley, is a senior account manager. The sisters bought the company from their parents in 1990, and under Karen's and Jackie's leadership, Frieda's has grown tenfold and now employs over 120 people.

It all started in the early sixties in New Zealand, where Frieda Caplan discovered an odd, brown, fuzzy fruit known locally as Chinese gooseberry. It was ugly on the outside but a sharp green color flecked with black dots on the inside. Its interior beauty and fresh, unusual flavor convinced Frieda that Americans would love what we now know as kiwifruit. And so began Frieda Caplan's quest to import exotic fruits and vegetables from around the world into the US.

Set the Direction

Frieda's sets its direction through clear company values and annual goals that are consistent with the company's long-term vision. The goals are communicated throughout the organization, and the various business teams focus on quarterly actions to meet their annual targets.

The company adopted a concise, direct set of core values:

- Respectful
- Results-oriented
- Collaborative
- Going above and beyond
- Staying curious

Communicate to Build Trust

Frieda's conducts quarterly town hall meetings where they share the company's progress with employees. In addition, Karen conducts quarterly listening sessions with small groups of five to eight employees at a time.

In both of these forums, everyone in the company is encouraged to contribute their ideas and thoughts. Karen and Jackie want to hear from their people, who often see issues with their customers or changes in the marketplace long before they do. The overriding message is twofold: everyone in the company is critical to its success, and each job makes a difference.

Track Metrics and Give Feedback

As a sales-oriented distribution business, Freida's is a performance-driven, metrics-focused company. Numbers and metrics are published and circulated daily. In weekly meetings, each manager discusses and explains results from the previous week, which allows the team to address issues and leverage opportunities in real time. This meeting is positioned as an opportunity to learn more about customers, trends, competition, and inventory. Questions are encouraged as well.

Anticipate the Future and Create It

Karen spends a lot of time focused on what's coming next in the grocery industry—now in the throes of significant change due to both consolidation and the entry of nontraditional grocers like Amazon through its purchase of Whole Foods Markets. Karen has a clear vision of where the industry is headed and how Frieda's fits in.

With its sharp focus on the future, Frieda's remains an innovator in the industry. The company was the first to offer prepackaged fruit and vegetable products, and it continues to add to its long list of unique products. To ensure the company's long-term success and viability, Karen and Jackie are working on plans that every business owner needs: succession plans, estate plans, and exit options.

Both Karen and Jackie are longtime members of Vistage Worldwide, an executive peer group company. As members of separate peer groups, they share ideas and challenges with more than a dozen executives from diverse industries during monthly, all-day meetings. Being able to draw on the experiences and insights of owners and executives of other successful companies helps Karen and Jackie stay ahead of the curve in their industry.

Attract, Hire, and Coach Winners

The two sisters are adamant about the importance of having the right team members on board. Karen describes their hiring approach as "never settling."

First, they define the position they need to create or fill and document the roles and responsibilities of the employee they'll seek. Then they identify the skills and experience that the incumbent must possess to be successful, categorizing the skills and experience as either "nice-to-haves" or "must-haves."

To narrow the pool of applicants to the small group whom they'll interview, they use the McQuaig personality assessment to compare the characteristics of each candidate to a benchmark. Applicants selected for an interview first meet with a panel of employees who best know the job the new hire will perform and then meet one-on-one with three of Frieda's employees.

The multistep hiring process allows initial positive impressions of the candidate to be confirmed and any potential flaws or lack of alignment brought to light during the individual meetings. At its heart is Karen's determination not to fall into a trap that many closely held companies find themselves in: bringing in more employees like those already on the team rather than stretching to bring in stronger players with complementary experience.

At Frieda's, onboarding the new team member is just as important as the selection process. Every new employee receives a binder with information about the company and an organization chart. As part of the formal orientation, the new employee meets with colleagues in every department of the company as well as in their own department, for an understanding of how his or her role both relates to the jobs of other employees and fits into the whole.

Build an Autonomous Company

To create an autonomous company, Frieda's worked hard to build a capable, professional management team. None of the company's key managers or department heads are family members. And although not embraced by all family-owned businesses, a formal organization chart sets out clear roles and responsibilities for all employees.

Frieda's diverse workforce is evenly balanced between talented men and women. All of the company's employees understand the philosophy that drives decisions about employee pay, promotion, and retention: at Frieda's there are growth opportunities for all good performers who fit the company's culture.

Celebrate Successes

Frieda's team meets as a group monthly to celebrate birthdays and work anniversaries. Whenever the company hits its weekly goal numbers, the management team buys lunch for the entire staff. In fact, all the company's meetings feature food. The message to employees is, "Even though this is a meeting, we're sharing a meal together!"

And they do all they can to make business fun. Creative, catchy phrases referring to the fruits and vegetables that Frieda's sells and distributes—such as "Superpowers abound," referencing Frieda's superfood, turmeric, and "Do it with passion or not at all," referencing Frieda's passion fruit—are displayed on signage throughout the company.

A peer recognition program allows employees to acknowledge one another with a star award. The names of those so recognized are announced at team meetings so the rest of the team can offer words of appreciation and congratulations for a job well done.

Chapter Two

Communicate to Build Trust

The CEO Tools Business System

COMMUNICATE • **E**XECUTE • **O**PTIMIZE

Trust is the highest form of human motivation.
It brings out the very best in people.

—Stephen R. Covey

As he set out for his regular morning run, Jack was energized by a new sense of cautious optimism now that he'd established a clear direction for his company. But challenges remained. Although his message about the direction had seemed well-received, little had changed in terms of employee behavior or sales.

Cresting the last hill, Jack saw a familiar figure sitting on the bench.

"Well, if it's not Jack! How are things going?" the man asked.

Jack told him about the One-Page Business Plan he'd created after he, along with his management team, developed the organization's strategies, tactics, and goals. They'd even set a big, audacious goal for the company.

"That sounds great, but you don't look very relieved. Why is that?" he asked.

Jack's forehead creased, and he answered, "Not much has changed. The results are the same, and I don't see people doing anything differently. I'm worried they didn't hear the message."

"Maybe they heard it," the man challenged, "but they don't believe it."

Jack bristled a bit. "What do you mean they don't believe it?"

"You presented a lot of new ideas and a fresh direction for the company. But many people don't believe what they hear until they see it in practice. How many times have they heard the new message?" he asked.

"Well, once I guess," Jack said. "The management team has heard the message more, of course. But we brought everyone together in a series of meetings to share our new direction and goals, and they all seemed to be on board."

"That's a great start," the stranger said. "But people have to hear things more than one time and in more than one way. They need to hear it, but they also need to read it and see it over and over again to be reminded of it.

"A friend of mine once said, 'Just about the time I can't say it one more time, everybody seems to get it.' He ran a very successful company. And another thing you have to do is build trust."

"Trust?" Jack said, his face red with repressed anger. "Are you saying my own people don't trust me?"

"Whoa! Don't get all worked up! I'm not saying they don't trust you personally. I'm saying they haven't seen any evidence to make them trust that you're committed to the changes you announced. You said yourself that things aren't going well—which reminds me what I faced when I took over at Snapper Lawn Mower in Georgia," the stranger shared.

"You ran Snapper!" Jack exclaimed. "That's a big company—an American icon. My dad had a Snapper."

"It was one of the most difficult turnarounds I'd ever been involved in, but we did it," the stranger said.

Jack leaned forward. "Tell me about it. What did you do?"

"We had to rebuild the company from a culture that was accustomed to losing to one focused on winning. For years, the executives had told the workers that they weren't working hard enough. I didn't believe it. So the other executives and I put on our blue jeans and spent time out in the plant to see what was really going on.

"We saw people who were working hard in a difficult situation. The plant wasn't well designed for their work. The design restricted access, which made the parts they desperately needed unavailable. By the end of our time on the plant floor, we'd eliminated enough bottlenecks to start the workflow moving more effectively and more efficiently. Workers felt like someone actually cared about them and how their work was done. It didn't fix every problem, but it was the first step in going from an us-versus-them culture to a culture of WE. *It was a step toward building trust."*

"One day in the plant was a good start, but it wasn't enough. By day's end, all executives and managers had reminders on their desks or walls saying, 'W4C,'" the stranger concluded.

"What in the world is W4C?" Jack asked.

"Walk the four corners," he replied. "It's a reminder to get out and walk your territory, whether it's the warehouse, the lab, the plant, or the offices—whatever makes up the physical working space of your company. It's a time to talk to people, check in, and ask what you could do better or differently. Ask them what they'd do if they were in charge. Ask how their families are doing. That builds trust. Trust doesn't happen when people are talked to; it happens when people feel they're being heard. Make it clear that you care, and show you're committed to a new direction and to new ways of doing things."

There's an old saying: "No news is good news." But in business, nothing is further from the truth.

Lack of frequent, consistent communication erodes trust. Intermittent, partial, or flaky communication fosters distrust. The levels of trust and communication rise and fall together. Building trust through clear communication can be one of your most valuable tools or, if ignored, can become the root of serious problems.

Importance of Frequent Communication

The absence of communication leads to what my friend Don Ray calls "Frog DNA." The head of a good-size accounting and advisory firm, Don understood the importance of frequent communication. Frog DNA refers to a scene in the movie *Jurassic Park*. In the movie, geneticist Dr. Henry Wu attempted to create dinosaurs from DNA recovered from fossilized remains. The recovered DNA was incomplete, so Dr. Wu filled in the gaps with the DNA from a frog.

The substitution worked to create the dinosaurs, but it also allowed the creatures to do the one thing that was never to be permitted: reproduce. The frog DNA allowed some of the females to change their sex to males and breed, causing catastrophic effects.

When we don't communicate frequently and effectively with our teams, they fill in the storyline with their own version of frog DNA: rumors, speculation, and assumptions. And just like in the movie, these substitutions can lead to catastrophic outcomes.

Often when the mind doesn't know, it assumes a potentially negative outcome or intention. And when we assume the negative, we become suspicious. In turn, that suspicion leads to a lack of trust.

This bad cycle has an easy answer: communicate frequently and work to build trust. Although it's a simple solution, it's rarely practiced by most management teams.

Business writer Brian McDermott underscored the importance of building trust when he said that "86 percent of employees say that the lack of trust stops them from doing their best." What a staggering statistic! Eighty-six percent of people aren't willing to put forward any discretionary effort because they don't trust management.

Discretionary effort is the level of effort that people could give if they *wanted* to, above and beyond what they have to do. A big advantage for high-performing companies is that people choose to give that discretionary effort.

The messages you want to get across must be repeated, especially messages about things that seem obvious to you as the company's leader. Suppose you have a goal to grow sales from $60 million to $100 million over the next three years. You hold a big meeting to announce the goal and discuss the plans. Everyone seems to understand and support the goal, and to be excited to make it happen.

But what if you don't mention the goal again during the next six months? You may see a lot of shrugging shoulders when you walk the four corners and ask, "What's our main corporate goal? What are we trying to accomplish?" A few employees might vaguely remember the $100 million goal, but they very well might think you didn't really mean it; after all, they haven't heard a word about it for six months.

The example of GAC, which turned its first-quarter performance around by getting employees on board a big, audacious goal, illustrates how targeted, repetitive communication can get the job done.

Tools to Build Trust

Here are some tools and behaviors for improving communication and building trust. If you spend time every day building relationships with your people, you'll be amazed at the improvement in trust and communication levels.

Walk the Talk

In July 2017, *Inc.* magazine reported that Dropbox chief executive Drew Houston was annoyed because his employees were showing up later and later to start their workday. So he scheduled an all-hands meeting to address the issue. On the day of the meeting, Houston had transportation problems and arrived two minutes late to the meeting. After the meeting, an employee confronted Houston, who didn't understand why the employee was making a big deal about his late arrival.

Finally, Houston came to understand that the problem wasn't that he was two minutes late. Instead, the problem was that he'd demonstrated that the rules didn't apply to him. It showed that he didn't respect the team.

"We can write down all the pretty words about our culture and our values that we want," Houston told *Inc.*, "but people pay a thousand times more attention to what you do as a leader."

Values: The Tools That Align Everyone for Success

Johnson & Johnson's values statement, called Our Credo, led the company through the Tylenol poisoning crisis in the early eighties, and J&J's performance during this crisis still stands as one of the best examples of corporate responsibility and response to a critical issue. Many believe it was the company's commitment to its underlying core values that created the clarity needed in this situation.

Johnson & Johnson's credo—which underscores its commitment to employees, the communities in which it participates, and its shareholders—begins like this:

> *We believe our first responsibility is to the doctors, nurses, and patients; to mothers and fathers and all others who use our products and services.*

Clayton Christensen, the author of *The Innovator's Dilemma* and *Disruptive Innovation*, defines values this way: Values are the standards by which employees of an organization make decisions about how to allocate scarce resources. Whether a company generates $2 million, $20 million, or $200 million, it has the same scarce resources: time, energy, and money.

We can expand the definition of values to say that values are the standard that measures what either gets praised and appreciated or gets condemned and punished.

It's important to clearly define what *values* means for your company. Here's a model for thinking about how values function as a key driver in your company. In this model, four sets of drivers create results in business:

- **Business drivers**—Most companies start with the founder's vision as the business driver. It leads to processes like creating a product and selling it, which in turn lead to results like sales growth and profit dollars.

- **Emotional drivers**—The emotional driver consists of an underlying passion for the business, product, or customer, which in turn generates communication about those things, again generating results.

- **Factual drivers**—Factual drivers are the numbers but, more importantly, the tracking mechanisms that provide ongoing feedback that causes people to get results.

- **Belief drivers**—Belief drivers are the unique values that each individual brings to the organization, which drive their behaviors and either get results or don't. Belief drivers are usually ignored by management, perhaps because we think we can simply post our values on a wall plaque and they'll be embraced. That's not enough. We must teach our values, use them, tell stories about them, and make them a part of what makes things happen in our business.

When CPA-led advisory firm Aprio, based in Atlanta, Georgia, set its values, the company created thirty-three fundamental statements about who they are and how they act. It invested more than six months to reinforce these concepts. The chief executive and the leadership team introduced the fundamentals in conjunction with the HR team. Every week, the company presented one of the fundamental values to employees. Included in the presentation were real-world examples and quizzes to make sure the concept of the week was clearly understood.

To identify your company values—or refresh them, if needed—you can use the Values Identification Tool. Gather your people together in groups of no more than twenty to twenty-five. Ask them to share what they think the company's core values are. Define *values* as those things that are most important to the organization or the team. Record the answers in a vertical column on a flip chart.

When all responses have been written down, each one will compete against all the others, like in a tournament bracket.

Values Identification Exercise

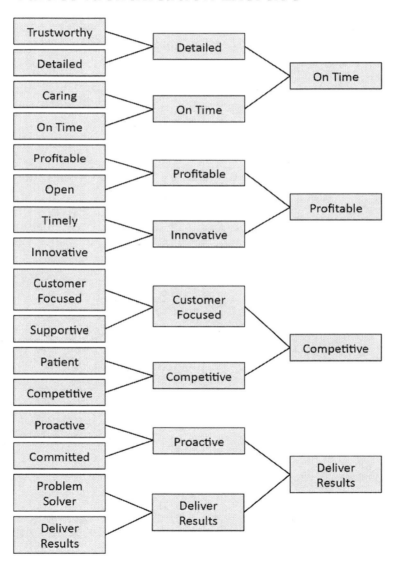

In the example on page 34, there are sixteen words in the first round. You may have more words to start.

Here's how it works:

- Compare each word to the next one in the list.

- Vote on which word is a better description of a company value. Write the winning word in a new column to the right of the first column.

- After the first round, any eliminated words may be added back by suggestion of the group.

- In the next round, compare the adjacent words again. After this round, words can be added back only by a majority vote.

- In the third round, compare the adjacent words again. After this and any subsequent rounds, words can be added back only by a unanimous vote.

- The exercise is complete when there are five or six words remaining. These are your core values.

The next step is to define each word and its practical application in the company.

Walk the Four Corners

One of the simplest ways to build trust is to interact with everyone in your organization—not just your direct reports, but the front-line people as well as those at the bottom of the organization chart. Because these valuable employees work day in and day out on the front line, they probably have answers to just about any problem that arises in or about your business. It's very likely that they think of opportunities that you may not have considered. The problem, however, is that they usually won't tell you what they know unless you ask.

So ask. Every day, get out of your office and spend at least twenty minutes walking the four corners (W4C). Stop and chat with one person, two at most, and ask open-ended questions: What do you see that I may not see? How can we make this better for our customers? How can we improve productivity in this area? How can we grow faster? Then stand back and listen.

All too often, we don't ask for input. Or worse, we assume the people on the lower rungs of the company don't use their brains.

> Jack Welch, the sometimes controversial CEO of GE, learned this lesson firsthand when he toured an appliance manufacturing plant in Kentucky. After stopping to speak to a manufacturing line employee, he asked the kinds of questions suggested above. To Welch's amazement, he got great feedback and excellent ideas.
>
> When Welch thanked the employee and told him how much he appreciated his candid feedback, the man replied, "You know what the sad part is? For thirty years you paid me for my hands, and all those years you could have had my brains for free."

Don't forget to include your customers and suppliers via a virtual walk around the four corners. They'll tell you more about your business than you ever dreamed.

And like Jack Welch, who visited a manufacturing facility far from his corporate office, don't overlook employees at remote offices or facilities. Schedule periodic calls, visits, and virtual meetings to get their input as well. Often, employees in the field, who are far from corporate discussions and planning, see what others can't or don't.

Intel founder and chief executive Andy Grove made it a habit to regularly phone the sales people farthest from the corporate headquarters to chat. "The snow always melts first on the edges," Grove said in explaining this practice.

As these examples of two top executives show, walking the four corners—both physically and remotely—can be your best tool for gathering business intelligence of all kinds and for staying in touch with parts of your business that are often unseen or overlooked.

● ● ●

Snapper Lawn Mower had been losing money for eighteen successive months when Kraig Kramers assumed the top spot. During his first week on the job, he walked the four corners, asking, "How do we get this turned around, wound up, and going again?"

To Kramers's delight, employees shared their insights on how to crank it up and start making money again. Forty-five days later, the company had its first profitable month and was on its way to a profitable future.

The company's employees knew what needed to be done and wanted to be a part of it. All that was missing was someone to ask them, listen to them, and then coordinate the effort to implement the changes they suggested.

3-by-5-Inch Index Cards

Sam Walton, founder and former chief executive of Wal-Mart, Inc., knows the power of a 3-by-5-inch index card. Walton and his top team always visited their stores throughout the week—a practice that continues today. The average Wal-Mart executive travels over two hundred days a year, visiting two or more stores each day.

Walton received a lot of feedback as he toured the stores— ideas, suggestions, and sometimes complaints. He carried a pack of 3-by-5-inch index cards with him and wrote down every bit of feedback he received. Then, at 7:00 a.m. Saturday management meetings, Walton pulled out those cards and shared what he'd been told, who had told him, and the employee's location at the particular store. The team evaluated the feedback and assigned tasks for action and follow-up. As you might guess, the Wal-Mart managers who attended these meetings began using Walton's index-card system as well, and their store visits became much more effective.

I've done this myself, with good results. In addition to keeping my memory fresh, there was a rewarding bonus effect. When an employee or associate gave me feedback or presented an idea to me, I'd stop and fish out my stack of cards. The employee would wait patiently to see what I was doing and then display amazement and pleasure while I wrote down the idea—as if it were the most important thing to me. And at that moment, it was.

Be Fully Present

It's all too easy to slip into the habit of not being fully present. When someone tells us something we think we've already heard, our minds can drift elsewhere. But this behavior—whether conscious or unconscious—can send a subtle but critical message to our employees and then infect the entire organization.

Say you're sitting in your office, working at your computer. Someone comes to your door and asks, "Hey, can I talk to you for a minute?" Engrossed in your work, you barely look up, responding, "I'm in the middle of a big project. Can you come back later?"

You just sent an indelible message—although unintentionally—that no one should interrupt you when you're busy. If you'd broken away from your work for thirty seconds, you could have determined if you were needed for only a minute. If so, you could have immediately invested that minute in being responsive to a valued employee. If a longer conversation was required, you could have set an appointment to meet at a mutually convenient time.

We unconsciously send these kinds of negative messages every day, and they can undermine trust and do other kinds of damage to our employee relationships and the company's bottom line. Changing our behavior starts with being aware of the effect our words and actions, including our body language, may have on employees.

To be fully present, stop what you're doing, make eye contact with the other person, and listen. This is how you send a message that enhances communication and builds trust.

Although we may never achieve perfection, there's no question that we can move the needle dramatically in the right direction. Our employees, understandably, pay close attention to what we say and do. To communicate effectively, we need to be sensitive to the effects that our behavior and communications have on our employees. Then we can be fully present, as *any* leader in *any* setting should be.

• • •

In each of its ninety-four years in business, GAC had lost money in its first fiscal quarter, April through June. No matter what management had tried or how hard the team had worked, the business was seasonal, and this quarter was their slow time. But in the company's ninety-fifth year, it turned in a profitable first-quarter performance. Here's how it happened.

The management team set a first-quarter goal to make $1.00 profit. That's a very small number to be sure, but it was a big swing from the nearly $750,000 the company had lost the previous year's first quarter. By the end of that quarter, they'd achieved—and even exceeded—the goal. The company accomplished this stupendous turnaround through *repetitive communication*—by telling a consistent story to all of its stakeholders and keeping its people focused on the goal.

First, the company communicated the goal in simple, direct terms. The mantra for the goal was Q1 = $1. Company leaders would hold up a one-dollar bill and say, "Q1 equals one dollar!"

That was just the beginning of the communication effort. Before the quarter began, the company sent letters to all its customers, suppliers, and employees, sharing the goal and asking for help to achieve it. One client, Victoria's Secret, gave GAC a $500,000 print job simply because a GAC sales rep had shared the Q1 = $1 message with the lingerie company's print buyer.

On receiving the message, some suppliers gave GAC modest, but nonetheless meaningful, price concessions. And throughout the quarter, the company sent out regular cheerleading memos, letters, and a special communication—called Buck$—to its team to report on progress toward the goal and heighten the hype and enthusiasm.

The company produced large lapel buttons with the goal for all employees to wear. And signage posted around the plant, on office walls, and in every sales office kept the goal top of mind for the entire work family.

Thanks to this communication strategy, GAC earned $104,000 in April, $19,000 in May, and $124,000 in June—for a record first-quarter profit of $209,000. GAC reversed its year-earlier performance by almost $1 million.

The celebration began on the day of the announcement and continued for a solid month. The company provided catered lunches for the entire company for all three shifts. A huge sign on the front of the building and smaller signs throughout the plant proclaimed Q1 = $1 WE MADE IT! The management team walked the four corners as a group to thank and congratulate every employee, on all three shifts, in the building's 387,000 square feet of space. Q1 = $1 plaques were presented to key players, and thank-you letters sent to all employees, customers, and suppliers.

In every possible way, the company reached out to stakeholders with the message that their hard work and support had helped meet—and far exceed—the goal.

Monthly CEO or Manager Letter to Your Team

One of the best tools for getting your message out to your team on a regular basis is the monthly CEO or manager letter. Its purpose is to:

- Repeat and reinforce the goals and objectives month in and month out, so they become clear.

- Praise performance-producing people and thank everyone else.

- Keep everyone informed about business successes.

- Point out team members or whole departments that reinforced company values through their actions.

Be sure to vary the message in each month's letter to keep these communications fresh and interesting.

One-on-One Meetings with Direct Reports

A thirty-minute weekly meeting with each of your direct reports will facilitate communication and build trust. Schedule the time, and protect it like you would if the meeting was with your largest customer. And remember, the meeting is an opportunity to air issues and concerns, and build trust—not an accountability session. After you've had these one-on-one meetings weekly for five or six weeks, proceed as needed; but be sure to hold the meetings at least once a month.

Start by asking the employee, "How's it going?" Let him or her lead the conversation from there. When an employee brings up an issue, ask "How can I help?"

This meeting should be a trust-building time, so establish a relaxed, nonjudgmental atmosphere that makes the employee feel safe asking for help or expressing concerns. Your job is to offer support or allocate resources to help your employees achieve their goals.

If possible, spend most of the meeting time discussing nonbusiness matters. The idea is not to pry into people's personal lives but to form deeper relationships. Permit no interruptions during the meetings. And by all means, turn off your cell phone, and let the employee see you do it.

> Leaders should have a "servant attitude"—a term coined by Robert Greenleaf in the 1970s—when it comes to the efforts and successes of direct reports. Servant leadership turns the power pyramid upside down: instead of the people working to serve the leader, the leader exists in service to the people.
>
> Greenleaf believed when leaders shift their mindsets and serve first, they unlock purpose and ingenuity in those around them, resulting in higher performance and engaged, fulfilled employees. The essence of servant leadership is empathic listening, responsiveness, and building a community focused on growing people.

Weekly Update

A weekly update from a company leader can include news about customers, employee successes and milestones (for example, birthdays, engagements and marriages, work anniversaries), progress toward company goals, and standings on contests. It's an especially great tool in companies with remote locations because it lets everyone know what's happening throughout the organization.

Key to the success of a regular update is input from across the company. So get all your functional and department managers to submit timely information about their teams and team members.

If you like, the weekly update can follow a regular pattern:

- Week one focus: prior month's results

- Week two focus: top sales producers or revenues

- Week three focus: employees who've done fun and interesting things, for example, 5K runs, triathlons, or other competitive sports events; or employees who've devoted time to support charitable events

- Week four focus: reinforce the focus and goals for the quarter and upcoming month

Clark Johnson, who led Pier 1 Imports, wrote a weekly letter to all his associates for over seven years. This was during a time when the company was opening a new store every week. Johnson stuck to one subject: customers.

Personal Notes Home

There's enormous power in the handwritten word. Especially during times of uncertainty and periods of recovery, a brief note of recognition and appreciation from a company leader can leave a lasting impression.

You can simply write, "Thank you for [what the employee did]! I appreciate your extra effort for our company." You both know what the note means without spelling out all the specifics, and it takes only a moment to write.

You'll be amazed at the impact these notes have on your employees. It's a fun surprise when employees receive them, and recipients never forget them. And more often than not, these personal messages are posted on the family's place of honor: the refrigerator.

Mary Kay Ash of Mary Kay Cosmetics used to hand-write thirty to forty notes a day. Legend says the practice fueled her success.

Douglas Conant, formerly at the helm of Campbell Soup Company, is a believer in the power of personal notes. During his time at Campbell's—when the company employed 20,000 people—Conant hand-wrote over 30,000 thank-you notes to his team. He also had lunch with twenty associates each month to hear how things were going and learn what the company could do better.

Repetitive communication and regular personal notes have big payoffs. Successful managers and companies use these tools religiously to build employee trust and motivate their teams to set their sights even higher.

Top Tools to Communicate to Build Trust

- **Repeat important messages**—Find every opportunity to repeat the company goals and direction. Be doubly redundant. Being consistent and repetitive will dramatically enhance effectiveness. Repetition results in retention and then action.

- **Request stakeholder input on your values**—Start with your employees and use the Values Identification Tool. Sort the results to reach a consensus about the company's core values.

- **Continually communicate about your values**—Wall plaques of values are a start but not enough. Put your values on your website and incorporate them in the email signature blocks for all employees. Find different and unusual ways to communicate your values.

- **Use symbolism and themes**—Use themes like Q1 = $1. Broadcast the message and help others achieve it. Make your symbolism visible and frequent.

- **Write a monthly CEO/manager letter**—Get your message out to everyone in your company to build trust, teamwork, and results. People like to know how what they do is affecting the bottom line, so tell them what's going on.

- **Hold meetings with direct reports**—Schedule an individual, uninterruptible, weekly meeting with each direct report to create trust and develop the relationship—not for accountability purposes. Talk mainly about nonbusiness matters.

- **Issue a weekly employee update**—This communication shares information about customers and employee performance. Each week, relate what an employee did to live up to a company value.

- **Send personal notes home**—A personal note is an amazingly powerful tool. Send handwritten notes to cheer on employees and congratulate them for results.

- **Feed everyone's efforts**—Volunteer your personal support to each employee's effort to beat the goal. Exhibit a servant attitude when it comes to the efforts and success of your team members.

For Further Thought

- Are the values of the company understood and being modeled?
- How would you rate the current level of trust in your company?
- What are you doing to build trust through communication?
- What tools can you use to build trust?
- Does the level of trust in the company allow the most important conversations to happen or are people holding back out of fear?

CEO Tools Case Study:
Aprio, Atlanta, Georgia

Aprio, LLP is a premier CPA-led business advisory firm. Founded in 1952 as Habif, Arogeti and Wynne—and later known as HA&W—the firm rebranded as Aprio to represent its transition from a traditional tax and compliance practice to a modern business advisory firm.

The new name, Aprio, is derived from the root words for head and heart. Serving clients in today's complex business environment requires the firm to bring the very best of both *head* and *heart* to each and every client interaction—precise clear advice, coupled with deep, genuine care for the client's best interest.

Aprio has grown to be the largest independent, full-service CPA-led business advisory firm based in Georgia. For sixty-five years, Aprio teams have guided their clients to success by providing advisory, assurance, tax, and private client services across the insurance; manufacturing and distribution; nonprofit and tax-exempt organizations; professional services; real estate and construction; retail, franchise and hospitality; and technology and biosciences industries.

Aprio employs over 400 partners and associates in five locations in the United States, who provide their best thinking and personal commitment to every client and demonstrate a passion for their work that fuels client success. The team at Aprio speaks over twenty-five languages and serves clients in and out of more than forty countries.

Set the Direction

To guide the firm's future and deliver on its brand promise about being passionate for what's next, Aprio developed a multi-year integrated business plan. Created by leaders from across the organization, the plan was designed to achieve several key objectives:

- Promote career growth for everyone in the firm

- Make it easier to grow and operate the business
- Stay focused on company goals
- Remain in control and independent
- Create less dependency on individual rainmakers
- Attain higher client retention
- Be more team driven

To deliver on the long-term vision, the plan is comprised of four core tenants:

- Accelerating growth
- Creating a differentiated client experience
- Delivering an extraordinary employee experience
- Providing an efficient and effective firm infrastructure

Each component of the plan is driven by quarterly actions and outcomes that are reviewed at a semi-monthly meeting to ensure accountability.

Communicate to Build Trust

Aprio worked with David Friedman—author of *Fundamentally Different* and former president of RSI, an award-winning employee benefits brokerage and consulting firm—to develop a set of Fundamentals of Behavior. Friedman's leadership of RSI was based on developing these fundamental statements. Aprio developed thirty of their own fundamental statements to guide and inform the behaviors expected and encouraged at the firm.

Trust building is based on how ideas like these are communicated. Aprio's thirty fundamentals were printed on a card the size of a business-card, which folded out like an accordion. Each of the fundamentals were listed and had an associated description printed on the card. The firm presented one of these cards to every employee in face-to-face training sessions where they explained and illustrated each fundamental. For those unable to attend an in-person session, online training was offered.

Each week for thirty weeks, one of the fundamentals is presented and reinforced two ways. First, employees received a weekly email from the chief executive that reviews the fundamental for the week and gives his thoughts and examples of how it applies to Aprio. Second, a new learning module was distributed that reinforced the fundamentals and presented multiple-choice questions to encourage employees to apply the fundamentals to their own work for clients.

The firm's partners believe that amazing ideas come from all levels of the organization. When team members feel a sense of trust, they're more willing to engage and bring ideas forward that drives the firm's success.

An example of giving trust to build trust is evident in The Aprio Foundation. The Aprio Foundation was founded by a manager in the firm's non-profit group. The Aprio Foundation is truly an employee-led organization. The firm's partners can hold no more than 35 percent of the board seats and the Foundation has five open committees, which gives all employees a chance to participate. The foundation provides assistance to local charities and non-profit organizations.

Track Metrics and Give Feedback

Aprio relies on metrics to drive and improve performance. Team member satisfaction and client satisfaction are measured at the firm level. Per-partner revenue, net income, and net income growth are compared to the averages of the *Inside Public Accounting* Top 100 Firms.

Revenues and margin, based on cost of services, are measured in the *CEO Tools* Trailing 12-month (T12M) Chart format. Aprio uses a business intelligence tool linked to their billing system to create real-time data that makes the T12M charts available daily.

The T12M charting concept was introduced by Richard Kopelman when he became CEO. Kraig Kramers, *CEO Tools 2.0* co-author, presented the uses of the charting tool to Aprio's CFO, who immediately embraced it. Because the chart has the power to remove the seasonality of a business—such as busy periods around tax time—it has helped Aprio's management see trends that might otherwise be explained away as seasonal anomalies.

For five consecutive years, the firm was selected as a Best of the Best Firm by *Inside Public Accounting*. Aprio is also an *Inside Public Accounting* and *Accounting Today* Top 100 firm and was named a Top Workplace by the *Atlanta Journal-Constitution*. In addition, Kopelman was twice named as one of the most admired chief executives in Georgia by the *Atlanta Business Chronicle*.

Anticipate the Future and Create It

Aprio used the What's Next? exercise to predict future trends and challenges, including increased competition from traditional accounting firms and nontraditional firms offering similar services; instability in global financial markets; cybersecurity; changes in the workforce; ongoing regulatory complexity; and changes in the markets in which their clients operate. From that analysis, management determined that future growth would come from a multichannel strategy approach. By focusing on specific vertical markets and practice areas, Aprio intends to continue their leadership position as one of the leading CPA-led advisory firms.

Kopelman shared the mindset needed to lead the firm into the future by saying, "We are disruptors and leaders in a traditional profession. We delight in challenging the status quo. We are not afraid of taking calculated risks. If we fail, we learn from the experience and come back stronger. We are focused on how to best cross-serve clients."

Aprio devotes considerable time and energy to developing next-generation leaders and preparing them for succession as their partners retire. Professionals receive ongoing training to become advisors to clients, as well as experts in the firm's industry niche. By identifying partners who plan to retire five to seven years before their retirement, they're able to tee up high-performing employees who might be able to move into those positions.

Attract, Hire, and Coach Winners

Attracting the right new associates starts before these potential employees have even graduated from college. Partners are assigned as sponsors to each of the targeted schools and they build relationships with candidates who are attractive to the firm. So that the prospects can get to know them, the firm hosts an annual student leadership conference where potential interns can hear from Aprio's business leaders and past interns who are now full-time associates.

Over forty students enter the firm's intern program each year and are trained to do the same work that full-time associates do in their first year after college. The interns also work in small groups of six to eight on a project for the Boys and Girls Club of Atlanta where they teach financial literacy in the club's after-school programs. They also produce a video or report that shows what approach they took to the teaching and highlight its success.

By the time the internship is complete, Aprio has spent over 700 hours with the individual, learning about his or her strengths and challenges, work ethic, creativity, and teamwork skills. Over 90 percent of Aprio's new hires each year are sourced from this intern program.

In addition to attracting and hiring winners for the team, Aprio focuses on coaching existing team members. The coaching focuses on continuous feedback and is employee driven. This ongoing coaching approach replaces annual performance evaluations, and it provides ongoing and continuous recognition, as well as more opportunities for advancement throughout the year.

Aprio also has a formal mentor program and sponsorship program. The mentor program pairs younger associates with managers and above to enhance their professional development skills. The sponsorship program provides the firm's next generation of leaders with an advocate and participation into an Emerging Leader's Academy to prepare them for what's next.

All client service team members have a defined learning plan and career path to help them build critical skills and advance within the organization. The firm blends instructor-led live sessions with online learning to solidify key competencies.

Celebrate Successes

At Aprio, bi-monthly recognition events include the Celebrating You and Promotions Celebration. This gives all partners and associates a chance to come together to celebrate monthly birthdays, anniversaries, achievements, milestones, and promotions in a fun atmosphere.

Aprio builds team spirit through many other fun activities and events. An example is the annual Aprio Olympic Field Day. CEO Richard Kopelman officially opens the games, and Aprio team members are divided into teams that compete in a variety of events such as dodge ball, rock climbing, relay races, and tug of war. Team members enjoy the opportunity to come together to play, laugh, and meet new colleagues.

The firm also provides a flexible work schedule, and team members can work remotely at least one day per week. During the summer schedule, staff can work with their managers to create flexible schedules while still meeting the minimum forty-hour work week and delivering exceptional client service. This program allows associates to enjoy a reduced commute and improved work-life flexibility.

To allow partners and associates to feel a part of something bigger, Aprio created The Aprio Foundation. Aprio partners and associates give back to the communities where they live and work by serving on the boards of industry groups and area non-profits. The Aprio Foundation also provides grant writing assistance, education, and volunteer support to local charities. These efforts help local non-profits thrive so that they can continue to create a positive impact on our community.

In one event, Aprio employees donated both their time and dollars to a "food fight" to benefit the local food bank. Teams competed to raise money and groups volunteered to work at the food bank, as well as at a grocery/clothing store that provides food and clothing without cost to anyone who needs it. The teams raised thousands of dollars for this non-profit.

Part II
EXECUTE

Chapter Three

Track Metrics and Give Feedback

The CEO Tools Business System

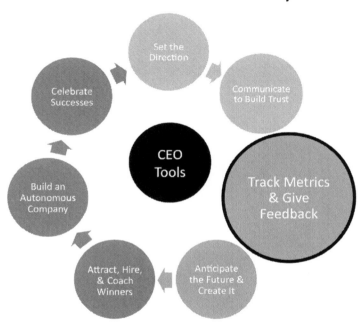

Set the
Direction

Communicate
to Build Trust

Celebrate
Successes

CEO
Tools

Track Metrics
& Give
Feedback

Build an
Autonomous
Company

Attract, Hire,
& Coach
Winners

Anticipate
the Future &
Create It

COMMUNICATE • EXECUTE • OPTIMIZE

I think it's very important to have a feedback loop,
where you're constantly thinking about what you've
done and how you could be doing it better.

—Elon Musk

Running was now a part of Jack's daily routine. He was getting more fit, and he felt good. And he found that he looked forward to talking with the man on the bench, although he wasn't always there. Today was a good day, Jack thought; the man was there.

Jack called out and greeted him with a smile.

"Look at you!" his friend exclaimed. "You've lost some weight and look strong coming down the trail. And was that a smile I saw?"

"Yeah, things are going better," Jack replied. "It's amazing how much more engaged people are becoming. I'm convinced they really want to help and are trying their best to achieve better results.

"And walking the four corners has been eye-opening for me and my managers," he continued. "We have very good people, and they have a lot of great ideas. Several people have told me that they appreciate my monthly letter, and some of my managers are even writing their own letters.

"And how about this: we even developed a tagline for the turnaround, as you suggested. It's 2C-30G, which means two new customers every month with at least 30 percent gross margin." Jack smiled with pleasure as he shared what his team had accomplished.

"That's great!" his friend said. "Mind if I ask a couple of questions?"

"Of course," Jack answered. He sighed inwardly, dreading the questions but well aware of their potential value.

"Now that activity's increased," his friend said, "how do you know if you're gaining momentum or losing steam as you move forward? And what actions will you take in response?"

The man continued, "Without tracking, you're just as likely to go off track as to stay on track. Two of the greatest killers of performance in business are, first, the lack of responsive tracking, and second, the resulting lack of anticipatory action."

Jack thought about their tracking metrics. He got the monthly financials from his CFO and saw copies of the sales orders. He wasn't sure what else he should be tracking.

"What should I be looking at?" he asked.

His friend pulled out a pad of paper and wrote: WGMGD. He handed it to Jack and said, "WGMGD means what gets measured, gets done. You've probably heard that before. Few things can have a greater impact on whether you achieve your goals than measuring performance and letting people know how they're doing against those goals.

"You've already seen increased activity because you've set your direction and communicated to build trust. Now you must be sure that activity is actually productive and is generating the results you want. People want to know how they're doing relative to the established goals."

"Makes sense," Jack said. "How do I know what to measure?"

"Look for areas that will have the greatest impact over time—areas where small improvements will give big payoffs in the long run," he answered.

"Everyone's watching you to see what's important," the man continued. "When you set a big goal that you want to achieve a few years out, it knocks people out of their comfort zone. It'll require them to do different things to produce this new result. Although people may say they've bought into the goal, they're still tentative about whether it will really stick. They may hold back because they don't want to be the only ones giving their all. So they'll pay attention to what you focus on to know whether this is going to be a serious effort."

"How do I send the right message?" Jack asked.

"That's easy. Just give them short-term targets that, when achieved, will lead to the bigger, more audacious goal," he explained enthusiastically. "Make it fun, like any sport where the overall victory is dependent on scrambling for every point. If you keep giving them feedback the way a coach does or provide a scoreboard in full view, they'll work to make it happen."

Consider these two questions: Are you gaining momentum or losing steam in your business right now? What actions are you taking in response?

If you can't instantly answer those two questions, you may already be off track. But you wouldn't be alone. More than a few companies have been in the midst of going public when they had a profit hiccup, an unexpected loss, or a major drop in revenue. Still others have been in the process of refinancing when an unforeseen event caused deep concerns for both the lenders and the owners. They were caught off guard, often at the worst possible time.

These headlines underline the catastrophes that companies can encounter if they don't have all the information they need:

- **Qualcomm delays IPO** for chip spin-off after reported loss (*EE Times*, 25 Jan 2001, 9:47 PM)

- **Box IPO Delay**: ...their financials shocked the market; in particular the scale of losses ($168M) (1 May 2014, 5:36 PM)

- **Massive losses and a delayed IPO** – here's how Spotify's headaches could spell trouble (*Business Insider*, 14 Feb 2017, 9:19 AM)

- A storage startup **delayed its $109 million IPO** the night before it was scheduled to debut (28 June 2017, 9:26 PM)

Measuring results is like taking a fresh look at the near-term future each month. We call this responsive-results tracking, and this tool fuels anticipatory thinking and proactive problem-solving. In chapter four, we talk in depth about anticipation as a tool. But let's find out how tracking metrics can help avoid these catastrophes and, even more important, produce profits beyond your wildest dreams.

Whys and Hows of Tracking Metrics

Can you imagine watching a football game that didn't have a score-board? Or playing a round of golf without tracking your strokes on a scorecard?

Of course not. Then why would you run a business that way?

> **WGMGD = What Gets Measured Gets Done**
> **"You get what you *inspect*, not what you *expect*."**
> —Favorite mantra of James Arogeti,
> co-founder HA+W/Aprio

It should come as no surprise that you've got to measure performance to achieve your goals. That's the clear message of WGMGD: what gets measured gets done.

As a leader, you need performance information to make a host of business decisions. And your people want to know how they're doing in relation to the company goals. Remember the second question that every employee wants to know: How am I doing?

To achieve your goals, you must track performance, measure the outcomes, and give your people feedback. It's that simple.

Here are the three steps, which you can think of as the "WGMGD formula":

- **Set targets**—Set target metrics for specified goals with your key people. Get everyone involved in determining what should be measured to ensure the desired results.

- **Track results**—Track results against the target metrics. This chapter presents a number of tracking tools you can use.

- **Give feedback**—Give regular feedback on the gap between the results and the target. Schedule appropriate meetings and create visual scoreboards that provide ongoing feedback on how results measure against desired outcomes.

• • •

Graphic Arts Center (GAC) had set an overall goal of growing sales from $60 million to $100 million in just three years—translating to about 20 percent compound growth per year in an industry that usually grows 4 percent to 6 percent a year. Following the WGMGD formula, the company established target metrics for milestones along the three-year timeline. As progress was tracked against the goal, honest, high-quality feedback was provided to everyone in and around the company.

GAC built trust by giving feedback at frequent intervals so that everyone knew how the company was doing and, more specifically, how *they* were delivering on their own part of the plan.

• • •

To make tracking most effective you must:

- **Measure the right things**—If you measure the wrong things, the wrong things will get done. It's best to focus on positive, growth-oriented measures, like gross profit return-on-sales or gross profit return-on-investment (inventory plus receivables related to a product line). Instead of tracking waste reduction, make the metric (and associated goal) positive: how much good product is produced using the raw inputs. Or track employee retention instead of employee turnover. Another idea is to measure profitable sales growth, not just increased sales revenues.

- **Measure only a few key indicators**—When you ask people to measure twenty or thirty indicators, it causes confusion. Settle on a few key indicators. For example, if the company is tracking thirty key indicators, break down the list so each executive or manager can track a manageable set of five or six targets. The multibillion-dollar company Danaher measures just six metrics to achieve outstandingly high levels of performance.

- **Provide lots of feedback**—It doesn't do any good to measure something if people don't know the progress that's being made toward the goal and their contribution to it. Be consistent and give regular, in-person feedback to tell employees how they're doing. Feedback can also be in a written document or update, or it can be displayed on scoreboards throughout the facility.

Tracking Tools

A wide array of tracking tools is available for your use. Select the tool (or tools) that you think will do the best job for you, try one or more, and be open to trying another tool if you're not totally satisfied with the results.

Quarterly Priorities Manager

The Quarterly Priorities Manager, or QPM, is more than a useful *tracking* tool; it's also a powerful *management* tool that will keep you and your management team focused on your highest priorities and ensure that you're on track to accomplish them on time and on budget. Perhaps best of all, the QPM is a simple tool to create and use.

To start, identify your top five goals/priorities for the next ninety days. (The time period is critical here, so focus on three months out.) Ask yourself, "What big steps will we accomplish over the next three months to bring us closer to our goal?"

Be sure to focus solely on the five biggest things that will carry you toward the goal. You may be tempted to list more than five. If so, you're probably looking at *activities* rather than true *goals*.

Here's an example of a first-quarter QPM developed by Graphic Arts Center:

1st Quarter

Graphic Arts Center
"PRIORITIES"

Name: Kraig W. Kramers
Title: President & CEO

PRIORITY RANK	CURRENT PRIORITY For Quarter Ending 3-31-xx	RESULTS FOR LAST QUARTER	NEW PRIORITY For Quarter Ending 6-30-xx
1.	Implement a plan to make Q1 = $1.00 that achieves $1.00 or more of pretax profit in the first quarter.		
2.	Get a $70 million sales plan written and bought into by quarter-end.		
3.	Meet 10 of top 30 customers by end of February. Visit all 6 sales offices and 5 suppliers in March.		
4.	Identify a plan for resolving the "slack month syndrome" by March 30.		
5.	Get our "key indicators" identified and tracking defined by end of February.		

After you list your top five priorities in order of importance, meet with your direct reports and ask for their feedback on your priorities. Tell them, "Here's what I plan to work on over the next ninety days to move us toward our long-range goal. Do you think these five priorities are the right ones for me to focus on and work toward during this period?"

Listen to their answers and take notes. Even if you disagree, write down what they say to show that you're serious about having open and authentic communication with your direct reports.

Next, give each person a blank QPM form and ask them to list their top five priorities for the next ninety days. Before you meet as a group again, coach each of them individually about how to get their priorities focused. Help them determine the right priorities for them as individual managers and for the company.

When you assemble your team again, after each individual has completed a QPM form with your coaching, amazing things will happen. Everyone will be on the same page and will understand the impact their decisions will have on the other members during the next ninety days. This is one of the many benefits of the QPM process. Even if your direct reports talk to each other regularly, they probably don't always talk about the interdependence of their respective priorities.

In fact, the lack of a common cause is one of the biggest issues a team can face. In many companies, each team member is running toward a different goal line; or worse, they have no goal lines. The QPM process establishes common cause—a common goal line. When your direct reports understand each other's priorities, they can act like a team and support each other's efforts to reach the company's goals.

During the quarter, you must help your team achieve their priorities. That's part of coaching them. Forward an article on sales planning to the sales VP who's working on a sales plan. Offer to help with analysis for the sales plan if that resource is available. Do what you can to ensure your direct reports accomplish their priorities for the quarter.

At the end of the quarter, fill out the middle column of your QPM form. This is your "report card" showing whether you accomplished what you planned to do during the quarter. This report card, or results section, ties a ribbon around the past quarter and finishes it off, furnishing a sense of finality.

Here's what it might look like:

Report

Graphic Arts Center
"PRIORITIES"

Name: Kraig W. Kramers
Title: President & CEO

PRIORITY RANK	CURRENT PRIORITY For Quarter Ending 3-31-xx	RESULTS FOR LAST QUARTER	NEW PRIORITY For Quarter Ending 6-30-xx
1.	Implement a plan to make Q1 = $1.00 that achieves $1.00 or more of pretax profit in the first quarter.	Plan and implementation completed: Q1 = $1.00 and in fact pretax profit was $200K!	
2.	Get a $70 million sales plan written and bought into by quarter-end.	Sales targets set at Feb 21st. Draft of plan completed March 5th. Plan finalized and accepted March 23rd.	
3.	Meet 10 of top 30 customers by end of February. Visit all 6 sales offices and 5 suppliers in March.	Customers met by March 30. Suppliers met by April 2. Offices complete on the 25th of March.	
4.	Identify a plan for resolving the "slack month syndrome" by March 30.	Solution is sales management and sales staffing. Will target a sales management plan for next quarter.	
5.	Get our "key indicators" identified and tracking defined by end of February.	Incomplete. Will be completed by the end of April	

Now, you're ready to list your priorities for the next 90 days in the right-hand column of your QPM form. One or two priorities might carry over from the just-completed quarter, but you may decide that they'll have different priority positions in the upcoming quarter.

End 1st Quarter

Graphic Arts Center
"PRIORITIES"

Name: Kraig W. Kramers
Title: President & CEO

PRIORITY RANK	CURRENT PRIORITY For Quarter Ending 3-31-xx	RESULTS FOR LAST QUARTER	NEW PRIORITY For Quarter Ending 6-30-xx
1.	Implement a plan to make Q1 = $1.00 that achieves $1.00 or more of pretax profit in the first quarter.	Plan and implementation completed: Q1 = $1.00 and in fact pretax profit was $200K!	Orchestrate April PTE = $50K and achieve Q2 = $1,000,000 PTE.
2.	Get a $70 million sales plan written and bought into by quarter-end.	Sales targets set at Feb 21st. Draft of plan completed March 5th. Plan finalized and accepted March 23rd.	Revamp sales management organization by April 30th.
3.	Meet 10 of top 30 customers by end of February. Visit all 6 sales offices and 5 suppliers in March.	Customers met by March 30. Suppliers met by April 2. Offices complete on the 25th of March.	Get "Project Swap" completed by the 30th of June, including one new sheetfed press up and running.
4.	Identify a plan for resolving the "slack month syndrome" by March 30.	Solution is sales management and sales staffing. Will target a sales management plan for next quarter.	Get AIC cost standards reset by the 30th of June.
5.	Get our "key indicators" identified and tracking defined by end of February.	Incomplete. Will be completed by the end of April	Get the sheetfed strategy refined and formalized in a written marketing plan by May 15th.

You'll use this chart to create a fresh QPM form for the next quarter. To do that, start your new QPM form for the next quarter by copying the information in the right-hand column to the first column of the form for the next quarter.

Notice the comment at the bottom of the "Results for Last Quarter" column about the incomplete fifth priority regarding key indicators; it was well underway and will be finished in April. It was not significant enough to carry over into the new priorities for the next quarter, and setting the sheet-fed strategy outweighed it as the new fifth priority for the second quarter.

Ask each of your direct reports to complete their forms for the new quarter by an assigned date (the sooner, the better, because the new quarter has already begun!). Then schedule another meeting with the group so they can share their completed QPM forms with each other.

During this meeting with your reports, take time to praise what everyone accomplished during the just-finished quarter. Be sure not to undermine the QPM's positive spirit by chastising employees who didn't achieve their priorities. Instead, offer a nonthreatening comment about what might have gone wrong and advice on how the priorities for the next quarter can be achieved. If serious accountability or performance issues surface, handle them in a separate, private meeting.

By focusing on the next quarter, while keeping the report cards on view for everyone to see, you'll allow peer motivation to kick in. Peer motivation is powerful—in fact, far stronger than superior-subordinate motivation. Remember: A rising tide carries all ships to new levels.

A couple of additional thoughts about the top five priorities. First, you probably shouldn't push this process down any further than your direct reports. If they want to use it in turn with their direct reports, that's fine. Some managers, however, aren't skilled coaches, so don't allow them to use the QPM in a negative way.

Second, top priorities are different from other types of corporate goals, so think twice before making them public knowledge throughout the organization. Suppose, for example, that one of your priorities is to reorganize the company or to relocate a plant or office. If people learn of an impending change before the final decision is made or before you've had a chance to communicate it the way you want to, serious morale and performance problems could result. Of course, your direct reports will need to know that you're working on an upcoming change, so they can help you with the needed plans. So the change certainly belongs on *your* QPM form—with a reminder to your direct reports that it is sensitive information that should not yet be in the public domain.

Trailing Twelve-Month (T12M) Chart

The trailing twelve-month (T12M) Chart identifies future problems and opportunities, giving you time to take action to fix things before they go awry or to move quickly and decisively to take advantage of a unique situation. If you can use only one tracking tool, it should be T12M.

This chart has many benefits. First, it's versatile; T12M can be applied to just about any meaningful metric or measurement in your company. Second, it's clear; no other tool gives a better snapshot of where the company has been and, more important, where it's going. Third, it provides a historical perspective, gives current clarity, and projects future outcomes equally well.

Former hockey great Wayne Gretzky said, "I don't skate to where the puck is; I skate to where the puck is going to be." That's what anticipating the future and making projections is all about, and the T12M chart will do this for you.

Many entrepreneurial CEOs and managers don't have financial backgrounds, and many hate numbers, dashboards, spreadsheets, and financial analysis. If this describes you, take heart. This tool is for you, and it will change your business life forever. Perhaps the best part is that your CFO or controller can create or maintain this chart for you. But it's critical that you check it on a monthly basis.

Tracking Sales. In his 2008 book, *The Breakthrough Company: How Everyday Companies Become Extraordinary Performers*, Keith McFarland discusses companies that achieved a huge breakthrough in growth, profits, and culture by making "a big strategic bet." In some cases, these bets put the entire future of the company on the line.

Imagine that you're contemplating a big strategic bet for your company, and you're relying on your financials to help you decide whether to take the risk. What you need to know is, can you bet on your current sales trend? Typically, you'd look at a few years of monthly financials to confirm a reliable sales pattern. But compare the chart of monthly sales figures that you might well use (at left) with the T12M chart built using the same sales data (at right).

T12M = Trailing Twelve-Month Charts

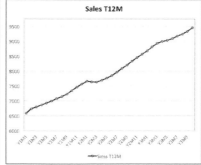

The sales data on the monthly chart on the left, which shows all the seasonal and other cyclical factors, fluctuate widely. But now look at the data plotted on a T12M chart, accounting for seasonal factors and quarterly aberrations. Seeing the strong upward trend in sales figures on the T12M chart, it's much easier to feel confident in making that big bet.

Now look at the chart below showing the same data over the same time horizon with the T12M superimposed over the monthly chart to show its impact.

Monthly to T12M comparison

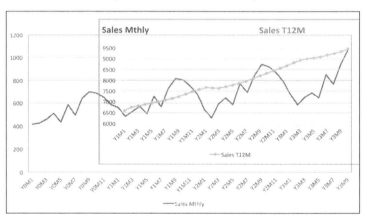

Here's how it works. Each dot on the following T12M chart represents the sales for the previous twelve months, ending in that month. It's a rolling annual total of sales data for three years, entered monthly, that eliminates the seasonality effect from the results because all twelve months are imbedded in each data point.

T12M Chart: Monthly Sales for Three Years

Example of Trailing 12 Months (T12M) Charts
One of the Most Powerful Tools ANY Manager Can Use!

CEOTools

HOW TO GET STARTED:
Example of charting 3 years of monthly SALES data on a T12M (Trailing Twelve Months) basis. You'll get a chart with NO SEASONALITY and every point is comparable to every other point. Look at this chart monthly to see things you never saw before about your business!

It's a ROLLING ANNUAL TOTAL tracked monthly. T12M charts will clearly tell you whether you're doing good or bad! Ordinary monthly charts often mislead and show little other than seasonality (see charts below). T12M charts also show historical perspective, a true trendline.

Use a regular spreadsheet software package like Lotus or Excel. Enter the month/year in Column B and monthly data in Column A as shown below. Then enter a sum function in the spreadsheet in Column C, Row 12: @sum(A1...A12) and now copy it on down that column. This is a simple 12-month sum that moves forward one month (and down one row) at a time. Then chart it on the same page using the spreadsheet's Chart Function. Better yet, enter your data in my Column "A" below (shown in blue), re-scale the charts, and voila - instant T12M!

	Col A: Monthly Sales ($K)	Col B: Mo-Year	Col C: T12M Sales ($K) (T12M chart)
Row 1	415	J-14	
Row 2	425	F-14	
Row 3	460	M-14	
Row 4	510	A-14	
Row 5	435	M-14	
Row 6	585	J-14	
Row 7	495	J-14	
Row 8	645	A-14	
Row 9	700	S-14	
Row 10	685	O-14	
Row 11	650	N-14	
Row 12	585	D-14	6590
Row 13	561	J-15	6736
Row 14	484	F-15	6795
Row 15	528	M-15	6863
Row 16	572	A-15	6925
Row 17	506	M-15	6996
Row 18	660	J-15	7071
Row 19	567	J-15	7143
Row 20	729	A-15	7227
Row 21	817	S-15	7344
Row 22	805	O-15	7464
Row 23	753	N-15	7567
Row 24	668	D-15	7650
Row 25	550	J-16	7639
Row 26	528	F-16	7683
Row 27	592	M-16	7747
Row 28	647	A-16	7822
Row 29	588	M-16	7904
Row 30	772	J-16	8016
Row 31	684	J-16	8133
Row 32	844	A-16	8248
Row 33	828	S-16	8259
Row 34	765	O-16	8219
Row 35	722	N-16	8188
Row 36	630	D-16	8150
Row 37	525	J-17	8125
Row 38	520	F-17	8117
Row 39	610	M-17	8135
Row 40	689	A-17	8177
Row 41	648	M-17	8237
Row 42	853	J-17	8318
Row 43	765	J-17	8399
Row 44	968	A-17	8523
Row 45	945	S-17	8640

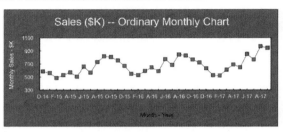

Sales ($K) -- Ordinary Monthly Chart

Helpful Explanation:
The figure in Col C, Row 12 is the sum of the numbers in Col A, Row 1 through 12. Similarly, the figure in C13 is the sum of the numbers in A2 through A13. And so on down the column.

Sales ($K) - Trailing 12 Months (T12M) Chart

Now look at your T12M chart: If it's going up this month, that's GOOD! If it's going down, that's VERY BAD! And this then requires IMMEDIATE ACTION by you to get more sales! Use this T12M technique to track revenues, gross profit$, gross margins (%), and just about anything else of importance to you. You'll be amazed at your improved success! Line up Ordinary charts above the T12M to see your seasonality, then work to "fill up" the troughs in your year! (See the true meaning of the two seasonal downs from the Ordinary chart on the T12M!)

The first dot on the lower left of the second chart, the T12M chart, represents total sales from January 2014 through December 2014; the next point represents total sales from February 2014 through January 2015; the next point represents total sales from March 2014 through February 2015; and so on. As you move across the page from left to right, you get a rolling annual total, shown monthly.

The T12M is the *only chart* that tells the truth—by eliminating seasonality—and that pinpoints where to take corrective action. By contrast, ordinary monthly charts track a single month at a time, going up and down from month to month without showing any relationship to prior performance. They give a very limited—often incorrect—perspective of a company's performance.

Even worse, monthly charts seldom provide information about a company's future performance. There can be many reasons that the monthly plots go up or down; some reasons are good, and some are bad. For example, if your ordinary monthly chart goes down this month, you might conclude that's not bad news because it dropped less than it did in the same month last year. But even if the monthly chart went up this month, that may not be good news, because it may have risen less than it did for the same month a year ago. The T12M, by contrast, shows you whether current performance is good or bad every time, taking prior performance into account.

It's easy to get acclimated to using T12M charts. And for the first time in your company's history, you'll see your revenues, profits, and any other business measures *as they truly are.*

Quick View. One look at a T12M chart tells you if things are good or bad. The good direction, allowing you to relax or nudge the data upward if you choose, is up. If the curve goes sideways or down, you know that you have a problem requiring your immediate attention. It's as simple and clear-cut as that. Moreover, the clarity that T12M provides can translate to a huge competitive advantage for your company—or provide your *competitors* with an advantage.

Say you don't have T12M, but your competitor, Company X, does. Every year during seasonal downturns, you think, *Here we go again, into the usual slowdown. I guess it's time to cruise through this slow stretch, maybe lay off a few people to preserve profits.*

But with T12M, Company X can clearly see the first down month of the slowdown and take action to see a future payoff. This competitor might instruct its salespeople to push harder to get a few more orders each week before the slow period, providing incentives or a special performance incentive fee (SPIF) as encouragement. So Company X will be positioned to see sales go *up* instead of *down*— and even to steal market share from your company.

Tracking Activities That Produce Sales. There's something else that's important to track on the T12M: what produces sales. In almost every business, the specific actions causing a sale to close occur at least thirty days before the month in which the sales dot is added to the chart. Think of these activities as key leading indicators (KLIs). By focusing on your company's KLIs, you'll spot potential weaknesses early enough to do something about them and enhance your company's growth opportunities.

That's what Guarantee Insurance Resources, an insurance underwriter, did. The company's primary KLI was the dollar value of quotes generated per week—which led sales activity by three to four weeks. Whenever this indicator showed the first signs of weakness, the company moved into corrective-action mode. The T12M chart provided a real-time snapshot of activity that had slowed, giving management a heads-up that the sales team needed to generate more activity to ensure its monthly sales targets.

By identifying and tracking your company's KLIs, you can determine how to drive performance for your company—just like Guarantee Insurance Resources does. Are your KLIs advertising or marketing dollars? Bids submitted? Marketing calls made? Employees on the sales team? Requests for proposals (RFQs)?

For construction companies, one KLI might be the total dollar volume of RFQs. For retail operations, it could be total dollars spent on advertising, emails, and direct mail pieces, or response rates to marketing activities. Using T12M to track these indicators and their corresponding results, you can identify trends and take action quickly.

Tracking Other Data. Here's just a sample of the other variables that you can track using T12M:

- **Income statement**—Sales and revenue dollars, gross margin percent, SG&A as a percentage of sales, profit dollars

- **Balance sheet**—Stockholder equity, debt-to-equity ratio, receivables turnover, accounts receivable to accounts payable ratio, inventory turnover

- **Cash flow statement**—Net cash generated (or used), net new borrowings, total credit line used

All these variables can also be tracked using another tool, the Twelve-Month Moving Average (12MMA) Chart.

Twelve-Month Moving Average (12MMA) Chart

If you divide twelve months of gross profit dollars by twelve months of sales dollars, you'll see your gross margin percentage. Because it includes twelve months of data, what is produced is actually a twelve-month moving average (12MMA), expressed as a percentage, which has all the same benefits inherent in T12M charts.

An example showing operating expense as a percentage of sales follows.

12MMA Chart: Operating Expense as a Percentage of Sales for Three Years

Operating Expense as % Sales Chart (12MMA)

HOW TO GET STARTED:

Example of charting 3 years of monthly Operating Expense % Sales on a 12MMA (Twelve Months Moving Average) basis. You'll get a chart with NO SEASONALITY and every point is comparable to every other point. Look at this chart monthly to see things you never saw before about your business!

It's a ROLLING ANNUAL AVERAGE tracked monthly. 12MMA charts will clearly tell you whether you're doing good or bad! Ordinary monthly charts usually mislead and show little other than seasonality. 12MMA charts also show historical perspective, a true trendline.

Use a regular spreadsheet like Excel. Enter the month/year in Column C and monthly data in Column A and B as shown below. Then enter two sum functions in the spreadsheet in Column D for 12 months of gross profit $ divided by 12 months of sales $. This is a simple 12-month sum formula that moves forward one month (and down one row) at a time. Then chart it on the same page using the spreadsheet's Chart Function. Better yet, enter YOUR data in my Columns "A" and "B" below, re-scale the charts, and voila - instant 12MMA!

	Column A Monthly Sales ($K)	Column B Monthly Optg Expense ($K)	Column C Month-Year	Column D 12MMA% Optg Exp % Sales
Row 1	415	75	J-Y1	
Row 2	425	75	F-Y1	
Row 3	460	74	M-Y1	
Row 4	510	78	A-Y1	
Row 5	435	73	M-Y1	
Row 6	585	82	J-Y1	
Row 7	495	74	J-Y1	
Row 8	645	85	A-Y1	
Row 9	700	90	S-Y1	
Row 10	685	83	O-Y1	
Row 11	650	85	N-Y1	
Row 12	585	89	D-Y1	14.6%
Row 13	561	90	J-Y2	14.5%
Row 14	484	97	F-Y2	14.7%
Row 15	528	83	M-Y2	14.7%
Row 16	572	85	A-Y2	14.7%
Row 17	506	90	M-Y2	14.8%
Row 18	660	85	J-Y2	14.7%
Row 19	567	93	J-Y2	14.8%
Row 20	729	91	A-Y2	14.7%
Row 21	817	102	S-Y2	14.6%
Row 22	805	114	O-Y2	14.8%
Row 23	753	128	N-Y2	15.2%
Row 24	668	102	D-Y2	15.2%
Row 25	550	99	J-Y3	15.3%
Row 26	528	108	F-Y3	15.4%
Row 27	592	109	M-Y3	15.6%
Row 28	647	102	A-Y3	15.6%
Row 29	588	113	M-Y3	15.8%
Row 30	772	120	J-Y3	16.0%
Row 31	684	122	J-Y3	16.1%
Row 32	844	121	A-Y3	16.2%
Row 33	828	118	S-Y3	16.4%
Row 34	765	123	O-Y3	16.6%
Row 35	722	119	N-Y3	16.6%
Row 36	630	115	D-Y3	16.8%
Row 37	525	109	J-Y4	17.0%
Row 38	520	110	F-Y4	17.0%
Row 39	610	121	M-Y4	17.1%
Row 40	689	126	A-Y4	17.3%
Row 41	648	129	M-Y4	17.4%
Row 42	853	132	J-Y4	17.4%
Row 43	765	135	J-Y4	17.4%
Row 44	968	137	A-Y4	17.3%
Row 45	945	135	S-Y4	17.3%

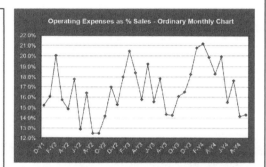

Operating Expenses as % Sales - Ordinary Monthly Chart

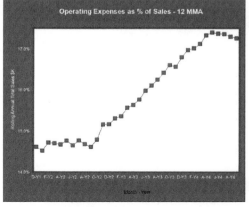

Operating Expenses as % of Sales - 12 MMA

Now look at this OpExp%Sales chart: if it's going down, that's GOOD! If it's going up, that's NOT GOOD. UP requires your immediate action by you to make it improve! Use this 12MMA technique to track gross margins (%), debt:equity ratio, receivables DSO, inventory turnover, and other important ratios. You'll be amazed at your improved success! Throw away all your other ordinary charts, as they will lie to you more than tell the turth. Only 12MMA and their cousin T12M charts always tell you the truth.

Sales Backlog Tracker

Some companies measure sales performance on a monthly or quarterly basis. But what if you were also to measure sales on a daily or weekly basis, to give you more advance reaction time? Number of sales closed, unit volume of sales, dollar amount of sales, number of sales calls made—all are easy to quantify and measure on a daily or weekly basis.

Two very effective tools for tracking a sales team's performance are, first, a daily sales report of orders booked (or entered by salesperson); and second, a weekly sales report that shows sales dollars both by individual and by region or product line, as well as the profit generated. It should list each salesperson's performance for the current month-to-date performance against goals, with a breakdown by product mix.

The more often you provide feedback to your sales force, the more frequently you can guide and direct them to reach the performance targets the company desires. Just as important is sharing with your team how their performance during the current time period compares to the same period last year. If your team does better this month than they did for the same month last year—and maintains that for the long run—the company will generate those coveted straight-line growth rate charts.

Of course, the other areas of the business must do their part, too. But continual sales growth can offset shortfalls in other parts of the business. And solid sales growth also tends to minimize the effects of seasonality in any business.

A best-in-class tool for sales management is the Sales Backlog Tracker, which projects results months in advance. The sample Sales Backlog Tracker on the next page provides a year-over-year view of the backlog for upcoming months. The key is to take action to keep your backlog of sales for each upcoming month larger than last year's backlog.

Projection of Year-Over-Year Backlog

Backlog Tracker Example

EXAMPLE

CEO Tools

Today's Date: 12/19/17

($ 000)   Updated each week.

Compares backlog for upcoming months as of this week at the same point in time last year. Permits apples-to-apples look at the future, so you can change the future! See "CEO Tools."

Booked Sales by Month

	Month	$ Sales Booked By Mo. This Year Thru 12/19/17	$ Sales Booked By Mo. Last Year Thru 12/19/16	Growth Sales $	%
	Jan '17	$7,030	$5,055	$1,975	39.1%
	Feb '17	8,365	7,065	1,300	18.4%
	Mar '17	8,537	10,991	(2,454)	-22.3%
	1st Qtr	**$23,932**	**$23,111**	**$821**	**3.6%**
	Apr '17	$8,186	$6,733	$1,453	21.6%
	May '17	6,532	5,438	1,094	20.1%
	Jun '17	6,137	5,776	361	6.3%
	2nd Qtr	**$20,855**	**$17,947**	**$2,908**	**16.2%**
	Jul '17	$8,230	$7,027	$1,203	17.1%
	Aug '17	8,952	8,408	544	6.5%
	Sep '17	8,583	8,288	295	3.6%
	3rd Qtr	**$25,765**	**$23,723**	**$2,042**	**8.6%**
	Oct '17	$11,070	$7,706	$3,364	43.7%
	Nov '17	8,470	7,322	1,148	15.7%
NOW -->	Dec '17	8,219	5,256	2,963	56.4%
	4th Qtr	**$27,759**	**$20,284**	**$7,475**	**36.9%**
	Jan '18	$8,794	$6,316	$2,478	39.2%
	Feb '18	5,954	5,805	149	2.6%
	Mar '18	6,168	3,527	2,641	74.9%
	1st Qtr	**$20,916**	**$15,648**	**$5,268**	**33.7%**
	Apr '18	$3,941	$3,734	$207	5.5%
	May '18	1,374	1,747	(373)	-21.4%
	Jun '18	502	1,274	(772)	-60.6%
	2nd Qtr	**$5,817**	**$6,755**	**($938)**	**-13.9%**

Historical Past (left vertical label, with up/down arrows)

Upcoming Future (left vertical label, with up/down arrows)

Using the Sales Backlog Tracker tool, you'll be able to decide how to influence sales further in advance. Without a backlog tool—or some other sales projection methodology that alerts you about a potential slowdown of incoming business—you lack visibility into future periods. Without this visibility, you have no opportunity to take early action to generate better results.

Let's assume the Sales Backlog Tracker report for the third week of December shows the next six months and your bookings for each month. The month of May might be your weakest month historically and show up on the report at $1.3 million this coming May, versus $1.7 million for the same month last year—viewed from the third week in December. Based on this information, you'll know it's time to take action.

The good news is that you have five months to correct the looming problem. With this lead time, you might well decide to ask the sales team to engage with their customers in December—five months ahead of what your competitors are likely to do to get May and June orders. You can create strategies and programs to give customers better pricing or delivery terms in the May-June period. Lowering your prices is a valid strategy during this weak season inasmuch as you'll face pricing pressure during this period anyway. If you give your customers the best prices now, you beat the competition when you do it again in December for your May and June orders.

Daily Cash Report and Weekly Cash Reforecaster

It's been said that an entrepreneur is someone who works seven days a week, fourteen hours a day, and is always running out of cash. This characterization is sometimes true, but it doesn't apply only to entrepreneurs; many professional managers run out of cash, too. The problem might be that they lack the tools to head off this problem—namely, a daily cash report and a weekly cash reforecaster.

To stay on top of your cash position, simply glance quickly at the daily cash report each day to see where you stand on total borrowings and your maximum available line of credit. Your "cash headroom" includes both available cash and the amount of credit available, and by reviewing the daily cash report daily, you'll know when this headroom gets too tight so you can make corrections. Perhaps you need to look at the days sales outstanding on receivables. Check into inventory turns and take corrective action before there's a cash crisis.

The Cash Tool for both tracking and reforecasting is shown here. Brief instructions on its use appear at the top.

Cash Tool for Tracking and Reforecasting

Cash Tool

Instructions: Issue report daily. Update the projection part of this report every Friday afternoon for as much of the near-term future as you can reasonably judge.

CEO Tools

Your Company Name Here, Inc.

Daily Cash Report ($ 000)

DATE	Actual								Projection					
	Receipts	Cleared	Net Cash	Cum Net Cash	Outstanding Checks	Loan Advances	Loan Balance		Receipts	Cleared	Net Cash	Cum Net Cash	Loan Advances	Loan Balance
01-May														
02-May														
03-May														
04-May														
05-May														
06-May														
07-May														
08-May														
09-May														
10-May														
11-May														
12-May														
13-May														
14-May														
15-May														
16-May														
17-May														
18-May														
19-May														
20-May														
21-May														
22-May														
23-May														
24-May														
25-May														
26-May														
27-May														
28-May		Holiday								Holiday				
29-May														
30-May														
31-May														
01-Jun														
02-Jun														
03-Jun														
04-Jun														
05-Jun														
06-Jun														
07-Jun														
08-Jun														
M-T-D														
Budget														
B (W)														
Y-T-D														
Budget														
B (W)														
Week of 15 Jun														
Week of 22 Jun														
Week of 29 Jun														
Week of 6 Jul														

Prepared By: _____   Copies To: ____ ____ ____ ____
Chief Financial Officer

The weekly report is a way to reforecast cash flow for the coming week using current forecasts, anticipated receipts, and scheduled disbursements for each day. It then includes the same anticipated transactions for each of the next four weeks.

Entering the actual transactions each day for a week and then repeating the exercise for the next week will help you learn your company's pattern of cash flows, improve forecasting, and build your ability to anticipate cash crunches. In practical terms, it will provide the information you need to manage cash inflows and outflows more effectively, helping ensure that your company never runs out of cash.

Top 5 KPIs: Daily, Weekly, and Monthly

Imagine having a set of Top 5 Key Performance Indicators (KPIs)—five daily, five weekly, and five monthly measures—that give you new, invaluable insights into what's happening in your business because each one measures something in a *slightly different way*.

• • •

At Snapper Lawn Mower, the team funneled five numbers to the top executive at the end of each day, plus five numbers at the end of each week, and five numbers at the end of each month. Even if the numbers didn't tell a positive story, he knew what he'd be facing the next day. That's what he preferred because, as you doubtlessly know, it's the unknown that keeps you up at night.

Snapper's Top 5 daily KPIs were:

- Daily cash amount

- Number of retail units sold

- Number of units manufactured, by type

  - Walk-behind units

  - Rear-engine units

  - Tractors, etc.

The company's Top 5 weekly KPIs were:

- Cash forecast for the next week
- Customer service metrics
- Sales bookings in dollars
- Where grass was growing (weather and seasonal patterns)
- Factory production cost performance

Snapper's Top 5 monthly KPIs were:

- Monthly and year-to-date financials in summary form
- Overall customer satisfaction
- Market share
- Progress reports on strategic initiatives
- Employee satisfaction index

● ● ●

What are your company's Top 5 daily, weekly, and monthly KPIs? What do you think your competitors' Top 5 KPIs might be? When focused on these key areas, any business is bound to perform better.

Almost everything we experience can be counted or measured, either objectively or subjectively. Although the latter may not always be accurate, a subjective measurement or counting is better than no information at all.

Top Tools to Track Metrics and Give Feedback

- **Quarterly Priorities Manager**—You and each of your direct reports set five quarterly goals or priorities that are tied into your company vision, strategy, and goals. The quarterly focus helps link the day-to-day to the longer-term, big picture.

Review the Quarterly Priorities Manager (QPM) weekly and share "report cards" with the team to broaden teamwork, better allocate scarce resources, and facilitate success toward your vision.

- **Trailing Twelve-Month Chart**—Use T12M charts to track sales and profit, and key indicators such as gross margins. You'll be amazed at how this tool allows you to see your business differently.

- **Daily Cash Report**—This tool will help you track cash daily and reforecast cash weekly, allowing you to head off a crunch, avoid growing too fast, and stay well capitalized.

- **Identify your Top 5 daily, weekly, and monthly Key Performance Indicators (KPIs)**—Know the most meaningful measures for your business and watch them like a hawk.

- **Communicate results to maximize results**—People like to know whether they're making it, so tell them what's going on. What gets measured *and* communicated repeatedly is what gets done.

- **Key leading indicators**—Key leading indicators (KLIs) are like key performance indicators, but with an orientation to future trends and outcomes.

For Further Thought

- What metrics are you tracking?
- How do you ensure that your metrics communicate insightful, actionable information?
- What measurement and feedback tools do you use?
- How do you track results needed for achieving daily incremental improvement and creating breakthrough performance?

CEO Tools Case Study:
Gibson, South Bend, Indiana

A key question every business has to answer is, *What business are we in?* For Gibson, the easy answer would be insurance brokers. The good people at Gibson see their role as one that is much more complex—as advisors and consultants. So, what's the difference? At Gibson, insurance is simply a *component* of risk management, not the *only* solution to manage risk. In addition to insurance, Gibson provides counsel and advice on complex business and people issues that go far beyond the scope of an insurance policy—an approach that offers their clients both value and sophisticated protection.

Gibson would tell you it's even simpler than that. It's about proactively identifying, quantifying, and managing risk. And it all starts with their purpose: to protect what matters most. In working with their clients, they utilize a number of tools to gain an understanding of what matters most. This leads to protecting the obvious, but also the not-so-obvious risks that organizations face, helping to ensure their clients' overall success.

Set the Direction

Gibson sets the direction for the company by developing longer range strategic plans, then breaking them down into annual tactics, goals, and responsibilities. On a practical level, they have a cadence throughout the year. They have a ten-year plan, and they evaluate what the next three years will look like. The leadership team spends a couple of days offsite to review major issues together and identify their annual goals.

Since its inception, Gibson's leaders have stayed focused on their clients, employees, core values, and purpose. They strive to develop a high level of trust within the organization, so they can have effective and challenging conversations, gain clarity around their most important issues, and learn how to solve them.

In fact, one of their major focuses is to operate based on input from every person in the organization.

Gibson's purpose is to protect what matters most, and these core values—which are regularly evaluated for relevance:

- Create a Great Experience
- Foster Collaboration
- Do the Right Thing
- Pursue Growth
- Own Your Future

They've never been afraid to change, adopt new ideas, or bring in outside consultants.

Communicate and Build Trust

Gibson strives to maintain open communications about the company and its direction, which is particularly important because, as an employee-owned business, they must build and maintain trust that the company leadership is doing what's right. They pride themselves on transparency and keeping people in the loop. They realize that people need to hear messages seven or more times before those messages resonate, and their communication methods include videos, webinars, in-person events, and email.

Further, they conduct quarterly State of the Company meetings, an annual State of the Company off-site retreat, as well as regular ESOP updates, celebrations, and off-site education throughout the year.

Track Metrics and Give Feedback

Because they're a client-centric business, Gibson's main focus is on three things: keeping the clients they have, expanding those relationships, and opening new accounts. They set metrics for each of these and review the leading indicators weekly.

To be successful, Gibson found it takes more than just setting annual or even quarterly goals. They set those, of course, but they also create metrics, to-dos, and have weekly meetings to evaluate where they stand in regard to those goals, which helps keep everyone on track. Additionally, they cascade the annual company goals down to each team and individual and determine what each of them can do to support the company's quarterly goals. In fact, every person in the company has their own weekly to dos, and each team has a scorecard that measures leading indicators, so they can predict future results.

They also created a "wellness index" that measures the financial health and wellness of the company, using the same key metrics their outside valuation firm uses to set the annual stock price. This is very important for the company since they created an ESOP.

Anticipate the Future and Create It

The insurance industry is one of change, consolidation, and acquisition. Realizing they must grow to keep the company alive, everyone at Gibson focuses on remaining relevant to their clients. For their employees, they strive for a demographic mix of one-third millennials, one-third Generation Xers, and one-third baby boomers. This is a challenge because the industry standard for millennials is only about 15 percent and is more heavily weighted toward boomers who have been in the business for many years.

To stay on top of trends and changes in the industry, they participate in two types of CEO and executive peer groups where they share ideas, receive very specific coaching and training, and learn innovative concepts.

Along with their annual and quarterly company goals, they've also outlined one-year goals and a three-year picture, as well as a Big Audacious Goal—where they want to be in ten years. They recently modified their leadership structure to give the CEO time and space to focus on their vision, major relationships, acquisitions, and talent recruitment.

Attract, Hire, and Coach Winners

Gibson is equally focused on the employee and client experiences. In years past, they talked only about the client experience: how to know them, guide them, and be on their side. But now they strive to do the exact same thing for their people.

A cultural fit is critical. Gibson interviews, hires, and fires based on their core values. They use a variety of assessments in the application and interview process to determine if a candidate is the right fit for the position and the team.

They target colleges that have insurance and risk management programs, and they've built relationships at those schools by serving on boards and helping with things like resume-building workshops and mock interviews. They attend career fairs and look for interns who will work at Gibson the summer between their junior and senior years. This gives both the interns and management a chance to get to know one another. If they both agree it's a good fit, that person is hired to work full time after graduation.

A few years ago, Gibson hired a number of millennials who relocated from their hometowns to work in South Bend. It was important to retain these key new hires once they were successfully onboarded and trained. Recognizing that these new hires had parents and significant others at home who might try to lure them back, they tried something unique: hosting a Get to Know Gibson Day. It was structured much like a college would when offering parents' weekend and was meant to introduce the new hires' families to the company, the leadership, and the culture. They even took the participating families to a Notre Dame sporting event, so the parents could feel the company spirit and camaraderie. A few parents left that day saying they'd love to work at a place like Gibson! One of their new hires had a big family, and he brought six of his ten siblings to the event—and one of his sisters now works at Gibson!

Gibson has always been 100 percent employee owned through employee stockholders. In late 2010, they also implemented the Gibson ESOP (GESOP). The GESOP is the largest stockholder in the organization, and every employee is eligible to participate. Through the GESOP, employees have the opportunity to earn additional funds for their retirement, based on the financial performance of the company. ESOPs create a culture of greatness and a high level of engagement because every employee is an owner. The GESOP is one of Gibson's biggest differentiators when recruiting and retaining talent.

Gibson was named a Best Places to Work, which not only provides them with useful feedback to improve the employee experience, but has also been a strong recruitment tool. Several candidates have said that they first looked into working at Gibson because they saw the company on the Best Places to Work list.

Gibson routinely receives honors and awards from local, state, regional, and national organizations that further solidifies the company's status as an employer of choice.

Build an Autonomous Company

At Gibson, all teams are tasked to document 80 percent of the things they regularly touch, in order to create replicable and accurate processes across their teams. Their goal is to elevate their leaders through delegation, which allows them to focus on the goals that move the company forward.

During weekly team meetings, the major focus is to solve any issues in a permanent and inspiring manner. They have a very focused agenda and a specific process to sort through issues. Gibson empowers their teams to identify issues and make decisions that impact their daily work to support a great experience—for the employees and for the clients.

Celebrate Successes

As an ESOP, success is a group event, and every one of their employees participates in the company's financial success through ownership. For every win they have, they experience it as a group through growth announcement emails where they share the details of each win.

Awards and recognition are key, and they have annual awards for both sales and service. Employee birthdays, work anniversaries, and milestones are recognized with a shout-out on social media, and there are opportunities for peer recognition. The CEO sends handwritten notes throughout the year, and client experience emails are sent to the entire company to recognize employees who have provided an exemplary client experience.

They incorporate a spirit of play as well. The annual off-site retreat is their time to celebrate the previous year, build excitement about the year to come, and have some fun together. Each October, they celebrate being employee-owners as part of National ESOP Month by closing the office for a couple of hours for a chili cook-off with games, activities, and prizes.

PART III
OPTIMIZE

Chapter Four

Anticipate the Future and Create It

The CEO Tools Business System

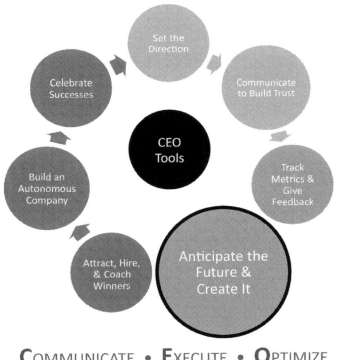

COMMUNICATE • EXECUTE • OPTIMIZE

> Planning is bringing the future into the present so that you can do something about it now.
>
> —Alan Lakein

It had gotten easier for Jack to get out his running shoes and hit the trails every morning. Thanks to his new GPS watch, he'd recently been tracking his runs and had improved his pace. He'd even set completing a three-mile run in thirty minutes as one of his personal KPIs.

As he'd donned his running shoes earlier, Jack had wondered if his friend would be sitting on the bench today. He was happy to see the man was there.

As he approached the bench, Jack checked his watch: 29 minutes, 49 seconds. "Yes!" he shouted, pumping his fist in the air. "I beat thirty minutes!"

"Hey, that's great!" his friend said. "It feels good to track your metrics and produce a great result, doesn't it?"

"Does it ever!" Jack replied. "And that's true on the trail and at work. Ever since we started measuring our business KPIs, our results have dramatically improved. Even better, it's fun for the team to beat a goal or target. People used to try to leave the office early, but I recently observed a group waiting after hours outside the accounting department for our latest sales numbers. When they got the results, they broke into shouts and high-fives."

"That must have felt good," the man said. "You've done a great job of improving your results. I have a couple of questions though."

Jack nodded in the affirmative but braced himself. Here it comes, *he thought.*

"Have you thought about how you'll maintain that momentum into the future? Specifically, how will you overcome future setbacks or obstacles?" his friend asked.

Good question, *Jack thought. He was already worrying about what would happen when the easier, low-hanging fruit had been picked and producing wins got harder.*

Picking up on Jack's change of mood, the man said, "I'm happy to share how I addressed those kinds of concerns, if you have time."

"Actually, I don't have time not *to have this conversation," Jack laughed.*

"I see I've got your attention," his friend said. "Now that things are running well, it's time to start planning for the future. I advocate a two-pronged approach: anticipate the best and plan for the worst. When you anticipate the best, you plan for the future in a positive way by using a What's Next? exercise," he said as he drew a diagram for the exercise on his notepad.

The business graveyard is full of companies and industries that didn't, couldn't, or wouldn't look at the future to anticipate what might happen and take appropriate action. Blockbuster Video and Kodak were one-time industry leaders who were guilty of this failure. And consider the hotel industry, the taxi industry, and the retail industry—all of which have been disrupted by nontraditional competitors and practices that existing firms didn't anticipate.

Think your company is immune to disruption? Consider the results of a survey of the leaders of more than 600 companies that McKinsey conducted. Eighty percent of respondents said they thought their current business model was at risk in the future. And only 6 percent said they were satisfied with their efforts to innovate for the future.

Plan for the Future

To plan and run a business, your eye has got to be on the future. Planning for the future involves three distinct steps: (1) create a vision that others can embrace, (2) develop a reasonable budget and reforecast monthly, and (3) use What's Next? to anticipate changes that the future might bring.

Create a Vision That Others Can Embrace

You must create an exciting, living, breathing vision that's relevant for everyone in your organization. Make your vision brief and concise, and keep it alive and flexible. With your key players' help, develop a One-Page Business Plan (see chapter one) to capture the vision.

Get your One-Page Business Plan in the hands of as many employees and stakeholders as possible. Consider sharing your plans with your key customers as well. You might find that they'll get on board helping you realize the plan.

● ● ●

Graphic Arts Center (GAC) decided to share its business plan, including its vision, with a key customer, Susan Rockrise, who managed Esprit Clothing's operations in some two dozen countries. To say Susan was a sharp executive was an understatement. In addition to her global responsibilities at Esprit, Susan worked with two of the world's greatest innovators: Steve Jobs of Apple Computer Company and Andy Grove of Intel.

After reading GAC's plan to become a $100 million printing company, Susan elected to give the company a $900,000 print job in one of GAC's slower months. She knew if GAC reached that goal, the company would be able to purchase the best printing presses in the industry. Recognizing how that strategy would help her own company, Susan placed the order to help make it happen.

Develop a Reasonable Budget and Reforecast Monthly

Your budget should be finished by the first week of each year—even before if possible. Finished means fully documented, accepted, and understood by everyone involved. Without a budget at the beginning of a new year, it's easy to get off to a bad start.

Once the budget in place, you must live by it. All too many companies treat their budgets like suggestions. After putting the time and effort into creating them, they never use them. Your budget is a critical management tool for keeping cash flow under control and profitability on course. So use it.

Track your expenditures and expenses monthly, and compare actual figures against projections. Create a regular monthly chart that shows whether you're generating cash or using cash—and by how much—on a T12M chart. Track operating expenses such as selling, general, and administrative (SG&A) as a percentage of sales using the 12MMA chart. (See chapter three for a discussion of these charts.)

But budgeting best practices go well beyond merely tracking results. It's critical as well to reforecast results monthly because it's easy for things that made sense when the budget was created to be out of line five or six months later. This means using a financial statement format that includes a column to reforecast your year-end numbers.

Reforecasting on a monthly basis allows you to respond to changes more quickly, which can keep brush fires from raging into out-of-control infernos. In addition, take a deeper dive into the results each quarter by conducting a major business review. Then debrief with your team to determine action steps to meet or beat the original budget and forecasts.

Use What's Next? to Anticipate the Future

A powerful technique to address issues and problems with your team and to keep the conversation centered on new ideas is to ask, "What if?" as part of a What's Next? exercise. Whenever someone jumps in to play devil's advocate on a new idea, simply intervene and ask, "What if it were possible? Suppose we could make it work? What would it look like, and what would be the outcome?"

The What's Next? exercise is a simple four-step process, illustrated graphically below, that can help you avoid being blindsided by competitors or surprised by changes involving your customers.

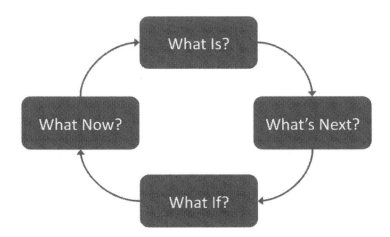

Step 1: What is? First, discuss the facts and the perceptions you have about the current conditions with your team in a dedicated meeting. What do you believe to be true about the marketplace, customers, competitors, your team, your company, and the economic conditions? Get everything you believe out on the table, speaking openly and authentically with your team.

Step 2: What's next? Taking into consideration all that's known or believed about current conditions, what do you think will happen next? Discuss all possibilities without judging their probability. You're looking for "black swans" that might totally redefine your views and approaches. (For more information about black swans, read Nassim Nicolas Taleb's book, *The Black Swan: The Impact of the Highly Improbable*, which discusses how an unpredictable event can redefine what is known to be true.) Is there a competitor, a technology, or a trend that—if ignored—could represent a disaster to your business? If anticipated, could it be a windfall for your company?

• • •

Craig Hughes, founder and chief executive of Total Transit, Inc., learned firsthand how a competitive change can rock an industry. (See his case study at the end of chapter six.) Hughes built Discount Cab Company into the largest cab and transportation company in Phoenix, Arizona. Then along came Uber. But by looking at how Uber had used technology, Hughes and his team were able to capture a huge share of the traditional cab business.

By considering Uber's operations, Hughes was able to identify a niche where technology could facilitate a significant growth opportunity: providing nonemergency transportation services for Medicaid beneficiaries who needed to get to their medical appointments. Hughes's new company, Veyo, uses real-time dashboards, GPS tracking, and predictive analytics to make cars available when and where needed.

• • •

Step 3: What if? Now explore how to capitalize on the challenges and disruptions in your business, industry, or conditions. In this step, focus on an issue that surfaced in the What's Next? conversation and say, "Yes, that might be true. If it is, what if we. . . ."

• • •

Barefoot Wine skyrocketed from being a startup to becoming the best-selling wine brand in the US in only a few years. To address the many challenges the company faced along the way, founders Michael Houlihan and Bonnie Harvey asked, "What if?" This question proved especially helpful in those classic good-news-bad-news situations that businesses often face.

In one case, a Barefoot salesperson had finally secured a large order from a leading grocery chain in Florida. Houlihan and Harvey gathered the entire company together to share the victory. The good news was they'd received a big order; the bad news was that, as a newcomer to the market, their product would be placed on the bottom shelf.

If you know retail, you know that bottom-shelf placement is the kiss of the death. Products on the bottom shelf are out of sight and out of mind. In addition, Barefoot Wine customers would have to bend over to lift the heavy 1.5-liter bottles that were the biggest sellers. If the product didn't sell, the store would drop it.

An audible groan went up from the group, but the two founders quickly began asking "What if?" questions to solicit ideas to address the problem. Someone half-jokingly lamented, "We'll be totally dependent on 'foot traffic' on the bottom shelf."

Over the nervous laughter that ensued, a team member asked, "Don't we have purple Barefoot footprint stickers left over from another promotion? What if we created a path from the parking lots of the grocery stores to our products on the bottom shelf?"

You may be able to guess the end of the story. When they put those purple footprints from the parking lot to the shelf, people followed them right to the Barefoot Wine selection. Sales shot off the charts, and Barefoot became a permanent part of the chain's inventory.

In the "What if?" spirit, Barefoot Wine also convened "awfulizing sessions" to leverage some people's natural tendency to worry and find fault. Whenever they considered new options or ideas, the founders got their people together to offer up every catastrophic scenario that could happen. Then they asked what was in place to keep the catastrophes from happening and what additional they could do to mitigate the risks. Were any of the fatal outcomes probable—and likely to occur—or were they merely possible but preventable?

It was this future orientation and thinking that helped Barefoot Wine become a leader in its industry.

• • •

Step 4: What now? The final step requires action. By asking "What now?" you ask what you need to do right now. These then become the next steps you take to ensure the company's future success.

As a company leader, you must be constantly on the watch for disrupting technologies that can damage your business. The What's Next? exercise requires your team to create strategic and tactical responses to a change in your competitive environment. The signs are probably already on the horizon—if you look and listen closely enough.

Tools for Planning for the Future

Anticipating the future is an integral part of any effective planning process. Running a business without planning and continual reforecasting is like driving your car with the windshield partially obstructed. The only way to continue is to slow down.

Your typical accounting reports are of no help, because they're like rear-view mirrors, revealing only *where you've been*. To help you prepare for *what's ahead*, there are seven planning tools for you to consider. Use one or more of these tools to accelerate your business to the speed of your choice.

Seven Types of Plans

Which of the following seven plans you decide to develop depends on the size, complexity, and nature of your business.

- **Strategic plan**—Your strategic plan covers the company's vision and long-term direction, and the evolution of the market. It identifies multiple opportunities and how the company will go about pursuing them.

- **Business plan**—Your business plan describes the direction, market, and resources of your business and how your goals for the year will be achieved. It includes action steps.

- **Marketing plan**—Your marketing plan identifies how your company will position itself in its markets and gain market share over time. It spells out the specifics of growth and market penetration, identifying how prospective customers will be identified, targeted, and reached.

- **Sales plan**—Your sales plan sets out the strategies and tactics you'll use to grow the company's revenues profitably. It focuses on how the company will convert prospects to active customers.

- **Succession plan**—Your succession plan addresses how new managers will move into positions of leadership. It identifies whether you have candidates inside the company who can lead the organization into the future or if you'll need to attract outside talent. Inasmuch as this plan provides a blueprint for if, how, and when the children of owners enter the business, it is especially critical for founder-owners and family-owned businesses.

- **Estate plan**—For privately held companies, your estate plan provides strategies for protecting and keeping the hard-earned wealth built in the company using tax, trust, and insurance strategies. A commonly accepted estimate from a study by Tobias Moskowitz and Annette Vissing-Jorgensen indicates that the average business owner has more than 80 percent of their assets tied up in the value of their business. Yet two-thirds of business owners don't have an estate plan or a succession plan.

- **Exit plan**—Your exit plan identifies how ownership of the business will transition in the future. It's wise to remember the saying, "All businesses transition eventually, whether by default or by design." Decisions include to whom the business will transition: children, employees, a competitor, or investors. There are many ways to create a transition plan, and each choice requires different planning steps in the years before the transition. Each plan can be documented on a single page and laid out in a similar manner as the One-Page Business Plan.

One-Page Action Plan to Start the Process

Plans are good first step, but they're of little value unless the key players implement them. Here's a straightforward way to start the implementation process.

Action Plan

ACTION STEP	WHEN	WHO	WHA
1.			
2.			
3.			
4.			
5.			

Step 1. Have a meeting with key people involved. Use a flip chart or dry-erase board with four columns: action step (What), target date (When), who is responsible (Who), and who holds him/her accountable (WHA). As a group, write down the action steps (column one) first and then complete the other three columns for each action step.

Step 2. Conduct regular meetings to review progress and update or add new action steps. Repeat this process annually.

• • •

This popular story illustrates the power of having a clear vision and anticipating the future. According to a frequently told tale, a young Fred Smith was in the last year of a master's degree program when his thesis adviser called him in.

"Fred," the adviser began, "we've looked at your thesis topic, and it just won't work. Your idea of delivering packages to people anywhere in the continental US by 10 o'clock the next day can't be done."

You probably recognize Fred Smith as the founder and chief executive of FedEx. He had the audacity to ask, "What's next?" and "What if?" Today, FedEx generates over $50 billion annually using a concept that was declared impossible.

But that account may not reflect exactly what happened. A gentleman who worked with Smith in the early days gave a slightly different account of this fable. Apparently, Smith was actually focused on a paper for an undergraduate class, and his idea concerned the overnight transfer of Federal Reserve funds from facility to facility to allow checks to clear faster. This, too, was considered impossible back then. But that's exactly how FedEx started—as the carrier of Federal Reserve funds—and it explains the company's original name: Federal Express.

Top Tools to Anticipate and Create the Future

- **What's Next? exercise**—Two of the most powerful words in any language that spark imagination and creativity, are "What if?" They allow you as a business leader to anticipate and address strategic changes that may threaten your business or offer incredible new opportunities. Try modeling different strategic scenarios, and then ask your team, "What if?"

- **One-Page Action Plan**—Assemble everyone who can make a goal happen and identify the action steps to achieve the goal. On a flip chart or dry-erase board, write who will achieve each step, the date the step will be completed, and who will hold the person accountable. Every quarter, gather the team together to review progress and set new action steps.

- **Four key business plans**—Create these plans: (1) strategic plan, (2) business plan, (3) marketing plan, and (4) sales plan.

- **Three personal plans**—Create these plans: (1) succession plan, (2) estate plan, and (3) exit plan.

- **"Awfulizing" sessions**—Assemble your team to articulate worst-case scenarios in order to surface concerns and identify actions to minimize potential negative outcomes.

- **Brainstorming sessions**—Bring the whole team together to work on problems or challenges. You never know which team member might offer the best solution.

- **Budget**—Your company's budget is a financial roadmap for the year. It's even more valuable when it tracks your company's current reality rather than your projections of what might happen.

For Further Thought

- How can you develop a vision for the future of your company and share it with your team?
- What are your target opportunities and when will you seize the moment?
- What trends, if they continue, provide the biggest opportunities or the biggest threats to your company's future success?
- What plans do you need to develop to prepare your company for the future and any transitions?

CEO Tools Case Study:
Mingledorff's, Inc., Norcross, Georgia

When you hear stories about fast-growing, innovative companies, the chances are that the companies were launched in the last five years. But Mingledorff's, Inc. is a fast-growing, innovative company that's over seventy-five years old. Over the years, the company has seen many changes, but it has maintained one constant: a commitment to serving customers.

In 1939, twenty-five-year-old Walter Mingledorff founded his heating and air conditioning installation company in Savannah, Georgia. Today, Mingledorff's employs over five hundred people and is a leading distributor of HVAC equipment. The company has thirty-three locations throughout Alabama, Florida, Georgia, Mississippi, and South Carolina; and with revenue of $435 million, Mingledorff's continues to grow at more than 9 percent annually.

Set the Direction

Ongoing strategic planning has enabled the company to consistently grow through both good and challenging economic times.

Chairman Bud Mingledorff, who is a believer in the power of the spoken word, has followed the curve of technology to communicate with remote offices. Years ago, the company built a sound studio, where Mingledorff recorded a monthly message on cassette tapes that were distributed to employees with a monthly newsletter. In these messages, he described the charts that showed the company's key metrics to make sure that employees understood them. As technology changed, the cassettes gave way to audio CDs. Today, messages from the company's president, David Kesterson, are delivered by Internet broadcast.

Communicate to Build Trust

When Bud Mingledorff began sharing company data with employees, some other company leaders were concerned.

But Mingledorff was adamant that showing employees in black and white that the company was a successful business was the right thing to do.

Mingledorff's continually looks for ways to reinforce their team and family culture, and the company's leadership is convinced that its culture and spirit—and the trust that its employees feel—are the reasons for its success.

Track Metrics and Give Feedback

After meeting Kraig Kramers and hearing his ideas, Bud Mingledorff recognized a kindred spirit. He eventually asked Kramers to join Mingledorff's board as an outside director.

Mingledorff's was one of the first companies to use the Trailing Twelve-Month (T12M) Charts, now a prominent part of *CEO Tools*. Among the key performance indicators (KPIs) that Mingledorff's tracks are sales (T12M chart format), gross margin as a percentage of sales, overhead as a percentage of sales, gross margin as a percentage of expenses, inventory, days sales outstanding (collection measure), collection percentages (a leading indicator), bad debt reserves as a percentage of receivables, inventory turns, online payment percentage, and online warranty claim percentage.

The last two measures—online payment percentage and online warranty claim percentage—track the company's strategic initiative to increase the number of payments and warranty claims processed online. These two metrics track adoption rates of these initiatives and give an indication of the success of the implementation of this part of the strategic plan.

Anticipate the Future and Create It

When a large competitor went bankrupt after the owner died without a capable successor, Bud Mingledorff realized the importance of planning for the future. Accordingly, Mingledorff's has a succession plan and has identified a strong leadership team to take the company forward.

Build an Autonomous Company

Mingledorff's has built an effective management team with multiple layers of competent professionals in place. Bud Mingledorff currently serves as the company's chairman, and David Kesterson is president. Bud and his team have been members of Vistage executive peer groups for many years. They are quick to credit these groups with many ideas that they've successfully incorporated over the years.

Celebrate Successes

The metrics that Mingledorff's relies on to keep operations on track are featured in a daily employee report distributed to 90 percent of the staff and a monthly web broadcast and newsletter available to the entire staff.

Monthly broadcasts welcome new employees, announce employee anniversaries, share metrics, announce top sales by office and region, recognize employees who have collaborated across departments, and share customer testimonials. Employees are encouraged to view the monthly broadcast with their families to learn about the company, its business results, and its initiatives.

Chapter Five

Attract, Hire, and Coach Winners

The CEO Tools Business System

COMMUNICATE • **E**XECUTE • **O**PTIMIZE

A coach is someone who can give correction without causing resentment.

—John Wooden

Jack had completed his first 5K race over the weekend, thrilled with his finish. In only a couple of months, he'd gone from being totally out of shape to finishing a race. That spark made it easier to lace up his shoes this morning.

When he reached the park, he thought about how well the planning sessions had gone in recent weeks. The team had developed the company plans for strategy, marketing, sales, and the current-year business plan. Jack had also met with his attorney and financial planner to lay out his estate plan, which included his exit plan. He was proud that the company's results were still improving and that he'd made solid plans for his and the company's future.

On cresting the top of the last hill, Jack was elated to see his friend on the bench. Sprinting to where his friend was seated, he extended his hand with a smile.

"Looks like you're making real headway on the trails," the man noted.

"On the trails and in business," Jack answered.

He told his friend about the progress they'd made in planning for the company's future. He shared that the What's Next? exercise had turned out to be fun as they "awfulized" potentially disastrous events and then discussed how to address them. Things were going so well, Jack said, that they planned to hire a number of new people, some in key positions.

"Do you mind if I ask you a few questions about how you select and onboard new folks? And how you coach and improve current employees?" his friend asked.

Jack thought about how they'd approached hiring over the years. Their success at hiring had not been good. He winced.

"Look," his friend said, "most of us struggle to pick the right people and get them started on the right track. We usually bring in too few candidates and use a haphazard process to select the one we like the best. My friend calls it hiring the tallest pygmy and expecting him to compete in the land of the giants." They shared a laugh over that.

"I've learned some things about how to do this . . . if you have time." Jack would have been late to his own funeral to hear his friend's take on hiring.

"Before you start hiring people," the man said, "do a little work up front. First, identify your top customer-impacting jobs. Not the people—the

jobs. This exercise was a big eye-opener for FedEx, one of my favorite companies.

"The first step is to meet with your team and figure out what your key customer-impacting jobs are."

Jack's eyes showed that he was taking this all in.

"After that," his friend continued, "put winners in those and other key positions. Set up benchmarks for these spots by asking, 'What does excellent performance for the customer—not just good and acceptable performance—look like in this position?' Then you can start to look for great players who'd fit those positions."

Jack had a question. "I understand how we should apply these benchmarks to new hires, but what about the people we already have?"

"I assume you're not talking about your star performers," his friend said. Jack shook his head no.

"Other than your high-performers, who you would love to have more of? Everyone else falls into three categories: high-performing but difficult to deal with; underperforming but well-liked; and neither high-performing nor well-liked.

"Let's start with the last category. Attitude and alignment to the organization must change first. Either their attitude moves up or the person is moved out. The people in the other two categories need coaching. Those who are aligned but underperforming often benefit from training and performance coaching to improve their results, while keeping them engaged with the organization. The high-performers with an attitude issue are tougher because we usually want to keep the results but not the attitude. Be direct with them about what you need more of and what you expect less of."

Jack nodded in agreement, very pleased that he was learning more about attracting, placing, and coaching winners. Their time on the bench today had been especially timely and valuable.

Build Your Employer Brand Proposition

To fill your positions with winners, you have to attract the best candidates. To attract top candidates, you must build your *employer brand proposition*—to convince prospective employees that your company is a great place to work.

In a 2014 *Harvard Business Review* survey, 60 percent of the respondent chief executives said the responsibility for employer branding was with them. Forty percent of marketing leaders agreed with this assessment, a clear indication that employer branding has gained strategic importance.

According to Brett Minchington, chief executive of Employer Brand International and a recognized global authority on employer branding, the answers to five questions define your employer brand:

- Why would someone want to work for you?

- What percentage of your managers have been trained in how to deliver your brand experience? (Employer Brand International research found that only 46 percent have!)

- What do your employees and candidates think about your employer brand?

- What do you know about your employees/talent pool?

- What percentage of your employees would say your company is a great place to work?

The last question is particularly interesting. It comes from the concepts in *The Ultimate Question* by Fred Reichheld. In the book and its associated research, Reichheld shows how much a single question can reveal: How likely is it that you would recommend this company to a friend or colleague? The question is meant to determine how likely your current employees are to recommend that others join your company.

As you evaluate how you communicate your brand, be sure to review your company's hiring process from a candidate's point of view. For example, many job searches start online, so you must be vigilant in communicating your employer brand on your website. What do prospective candidates see when they visit your website? Do they see a place where they'd like to work—where employees are valued and rewarded? Pay particular attention to your online presence on employee review sites like Glassdoor, Comparably, and Vault.

Next, check out whether your company's physical presence reinforces your employer brand by walking yourself through the interview process that candidates follow. What do candidates see when they walk in your company's door for an interview? Who do they meet and engage with during their visit? Would you be excited to work at your company?

The most important jobs in your company are those with the greatest potential to impact your customers and prospects in either a positive or a negative way. Without winners in those key spots, you're putting your company's success at risk. So take a critical look at your brand so you can attract the winners you need.

Identify Key Customer-Impacting Jobs

Would you turn over your car keys to a stranger without knowing his or her driving record? Of course not. So why would you gamble on the success of your company by turning over a key customer-impacting position to someone who might be all wrong for the job?

In fact, identifying the key customer-impacting jobs in your company is the most powerful tool on the people side of your business. And it's a critical first step before you even think about hiring another employee.

This tool helps you identify the top five customer-impacting jobs in your company so you can put winners in those key positions.

Start by brainstorming with your management or leadership team. Ask your team these questions:

- Which jobs have the most frequent interaction with customers?

- Which jobs have the most potential to have an impact, positive or negative, for our customers?

Using a matrix like the one shown on the next page can help focus the team's discussion.

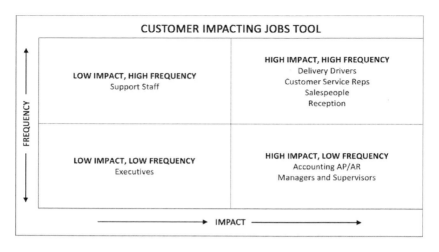

FedEx does a lot of things right, and its results prove the point. The company is consistently in the Top 100 on the *Fortune* 500 list and for seventeen years has been on the list of Top 20 most admired companies.

A lot of people at FedEx helped win these accolades. Some might say that Fred Smith, the company's chairman, president, and chief executive officer, is largely responsible. Others might say that the company's great leadership and management teams are the reason for its success. It could also be argued that the team of seven thousand that works from midnight until 5 a.m., sorting well over one million packages every night, is responsible for FedEx's success.

It turns out that the choice of a package delivery service depends on one FedEx position more than any other. I bet you guessed it: it's the delivery person that a customer interacts with at a FedEx office or warehouse—often twice a day. The most important predictor of which package delivery company will get the business is the employee who picks up and delivers packages.

• • •

Now that you've identified the top five customer-impacting jobs in your company, you must determine what outstanding performance means for each position *from the customer's point of view.* After all, you need the associates in those spots to be top performers.

To flesh out a list for each position, engage in a give-and-take with your high-performing employees who currently hold those positions. It may take several conversations to uncover what the top 10 percent do differently from everyone else, but you'll soon figure it out. Remember—you're looking for what *the customer* considers to be top performance.

Next, quantify the five definitions you've come up with. This may be harder to do for some positions, but every position can be measured in some way. Excellent performance for a sales assistant, for example, might be defined by the number of weeks the associate has worked with error-free order entry. An accounting associate might be measured by the percentage of invoices he or she has generated correctly. Both positions might also be measured by how helpful they are perceived to be by the company.

After you've defined and quantified excellent performance for your key customer-facing positions, take three steps to support and recognize employees who currently hold these positions as well as those whom you'll bring on board as spots open up:

- **Build a compensation system**—When an employee excels, he or she might receive a bonus or special performance incentive fee (SPIF). Payouts should be frequent—monthly or quarterly—so employees associate the bonus with their current performance.

- **Create a recognition system**—Ensure that highflyers receive regular pats on the back for superb results. Consider spotlighting these employees in your monthly letter to your team or another company-wide communication tool or forum.

- **Provide training and tools**—You're counting on associates in your key customer-facing jobs to deliver excellent performance, so you must shower them with the training and support they need to be winners. Consider special training for these new hires above and beyond your standard onboarding process.

When you've completed this process for your five key customer impacting jobs, move on to the other important jobs in the company. Using this approach, you can dramatically improve the performance of individual employees *and* the whole company.

Identify Winners

Mel Robbins, best-selling author of *The 5 Second Rule,* has this to say about winners: "So often we tie the word 'win' to an outcome, but what ACTUALLY makes a winner is what you do day in and day out to push yourself to become the best version of you."

Winners are not just better at one part of the job, they do every part of the job a little better than others do. But before you can hire a winner for a key customer impacting position—or any position, for that matter—you must identify a pool of potential winners who are a good match to your specific jobs.

To identify the kind of person you need for a particular job, write a *job specification*, not a job description. The job specification outlines the characteristics of the position and identifies the skills, knowledge, and abilities the candidate must have to succeed. It paints a clear, comprehensive picture so you know *exactly* what to look for when sourcing and interviewing applicants.

Include these criteria:

- Must-have skills and experience to do the job

- Nice-to-have skills and experience

- Amazing-to-have skills and experience that will set the candidate apart

Try to limit your must-haves to three or four key points based on facts or experience—or you may disqualify the entire universe of candidates!

Why not Google each candidate? You may learn some interesting things that could help you decide whether to interview a candidate. For example, you may discover that the candidate is involved in charitable activities, which you might count as a plus. Or, you might discover some things that could be detrimental or embarrassing to the company and decide to eliminate the candidate from consideration.

You might consider using one of the many personality or psychological assessment tools available. Some tests are more data driven and present the candidate in a detailed manner; others are more visually oriented and represent the candidate in graphs and charts. Use the format that you're most comfortable reviewing.

An assessment is not a tool to use to make a final hiring decision. It's most valuable when you compare the results of the assessment with your own impression of candidates during interviews. Some candidates are good at interviewing, and a skilled interviewee may be able to mask or hide issues that an assessment tool would bring to light.

Checking references is an important step, but don't expect to get much detail about the person. Today, many companies are afraid of lawsuits and have advised supervisors to offer only the barest of information about their former employees. Geoff Smart, co-author of *WHO*, refers to a technique he calls TORC, which stands for threat of reference check. Using this technique, ask the candidate what he or she thinks a reference would say if contacted: "I'd like to ask your reference, Mary Smith, about your prospecting ability. What do you think Mary will tell me?"

The TORC approach accomplishes two things. First, it lets candidates know you're serious about them and plan to ask their references specific questions (of course, a reference may decline to answer). And second, it sheds light on what a candidate thinks the reference will say. Both are very valuable.

For managers and other higher-level hires, it's smart to conduct a social interview. Take the candidate to lunch or dinner. For senior team members, include their spouse or significant other at a dinner. Observe how the candidate interacts with others, including the wait staff. Charles "Red" Scott a legend in the business world, said, "I can tell a lot about a person by how they treat a waiter or other service staff."

Strive to be a company with a great culture, and you'll become a talent magnet. Set your sights on being a place where people *want* to work and *love* to work—and your employees will talk up your company to your entire community! And don't forget to toot your own horn both loud and frequently on all your communication platforms.

Interview the Candidates

Once you've narrowed the group of interviewees, contacted references for the top two or three candidates, and decided which candidate you'd like to hire, you must sell the candidate on joining your company.

Here are four tools to help you make a persuasive case during the final interview:

- Have a great story to tell about your company.

- Have a compensation plan better than your industry.

- Offer opportunity for personal growth.

- Discuss your culture of ongoing coaching and praise and recognition, and tell candidates how communication, trust, feedback, and openness are an integral part of it.

• • •

Michael Houlihan and Bonnie Harvey, founders of Barefoot Wine, had a secret interviewer in their hiring process: their administrative assistant. She greeted and interacted with every candidate, asking what probably seemed like innocent, nonprobing questions. Then, after candidates left, she reported to Houlihan and Harvey how they'd treated her and responded to her questions.

Another business leader always had a car service pick up candidates for executive-level positions at the airport. Little did they know that what seemed like a casual conversation with the driver was part of the interview. The company used the same driver each time, and he had been trained on the questions to ask every candidate and reported back later.

Hiring Great Managers

If it's hard to hire great people, it's even harder to hire great managers. That's perhaps why current employees are all too often promoted to managerial spots because they're the best person in their department—not because they have what it takes to be effective managers. Making this mistake hurts the company twice: you lose a bright talent in the functional area *and* you've got a new manager who can't do the job.

But there's a simple, easy-to-use tool that can help you navigate this hiring challenge. The Managerial Success Traits (MST) tool is a list of personality traits and abilities that strongly correlate with success at the supervisor, middle manager, and chief executive levels.

Managerial Success Traits (MST)   **CEO** Tools

SCORE MANAGER OR CANDIDATE ON A 1 - 10 SCALE: Manager's or Candidate's
                                                        Name: _____

Enter Each
Scorer's Name -------------------------->   TOTAL
                                                                             SCORES

Personal Motivation
  Self-Discipline
  Mentorship = Is Coach and Coachee
  Risk-Taking
  Energy = Quick & Long Hours
  Expectation of Success
  Self-Confidence
  Healthy Respect for Authority
  Emotional Stability
  Green & Growing = Wants to Learn
  Enthusiasm
  Introspection

Business Skills
  Finance
  Marketing
  Relevant Business Experience
  People-Selection Skills
  Luck
  Track Results
  Focus on Customer

Decision Making
  Intuitive Deduction
  Problem-Solving Approach
  Abstract Conceptualization
  Balancing Results vs People

Influence
  Leadership
  Communication
  Organizes Self & Others
  Human Sensitivity
  Good Listener
  Vision
  Goal Setter
  Trust Builder

Intelligence
  Common Sense
  Street Smarts
  Judgement
  Academic Rigor = College Degrees
  Conceptual Grasp

Memory
  Long Term
  Critical Detail

TOTAL SCORES BY EACH SCORER =   0   0   0   0   0   0

The next time you need to fill a key manager spot, use the MST scorecard to rank both internal and external candidates on each of the traits. Discuss any low scores with the candidate during the hiring process. You'll know you have a winner if a candidate wants to talk about his or her weaknesses and sees them as learning opportunities. Winners don't pretend to be perfect; they acknowledge their shortcomings and explain how they're working on them.

Coaching Winners

All employees want to know how they're doing, which is why scheduling regular one-on-one meetings with your key people and direct reports is critical. The point of these coaching sessions is to provide feedback, give recognition, and assess what resources you can provide to help them accomplish their objectives. There are three types of coaching sessions, each correlating with the performance of the employee.

Coaching Session Type 1: High Performers

As managers, we spend so much time on problems that meeting individually with our top performers—employees who are ahead of their goals or who generally achieve their goals and objectives—can fall through the cracks. Or we assume that they don't need our help or that they work better when we just leave them alone. But everyone wants to know how their performance aligns with your expectations, so don't deny them this feedback.

In your meetings with high performers, you'll review where they stand on their top priorities, providing encouragement, support, and resources as needed. Chances are that the opportunity to meet one-on-one with you and to hear you sing their praises will spur your top performers to even greater heights.

Coaching Session Type 2: Employees Needing Improvement

A different type of coaching session is in order for your employees who, although headed in the right direction, are delivering below-par results or widely fluctuating results. Up and down performance typi-cally occurs when an employee is new to a role or when an experienced employee is having trouble adapting to changing market conditions.

In either case, you'll need to be more hands-on. In addition to reviewing these employees' priorities, ask for details on the tactics and actions they're planning to meet expectations. Confirm that they're working on the right priorities, and listen carefully to their planned actions before sharing your recommendations.

You have two opportunities in this conversation. The first is to determine if their instincts about how to address the issue are in line with yours. If so, wholeheartedly and enthusiastically endorse their plan and praise their insight. Your cheerleading will increase their confidence, and they'll attack their plan with renewed vigor.

The second opportunity is to test their will to take the action they've suggested. As the famous productivity author, David Allen, says, "There is a big difference between knowing and doing." So don't assume that because they have a solid plan to address their deficiencies, they have the resolve to complete it. They may need outside resources, for example, a contracted performance coach. Trust your instincts on this.

Coaching Session Type 3: Underperformers

Employees who are underperforming typically lack either will or skill. Employees who lack skill may take the right actions but not deliver the desired results. This could be a training issue. Something about the way they're executing might be blocking their success.

Consider the salesperson who makes the right number of calls but isn't closing business. There's almost always some technique—either its presence or its absence—that's causing them to fail. Training, role-playing, and joint calls can reveal the problem, and you can help put them on a better path.

A lack of will on the part of an employee is an attitude issue that requires a much higher level of supervision—perhaps even daily prog-ress reports to measure any changes in results. But if an unmotivated employee can't do the job *and* can't conclude that the job isn't a good fit, you'll have to make the point in clear and unambiguous language.

• • •

In an article from July 2017, by Gordon Tredgold, we learned that JM Enterprises is a company that does a lot of things right. After all, a company doesn't make it to the list of the Top 100 Companies to Work For if it doesn't do things right, and JM Enterprises made the list nineteen times.

When Tredgold asked how JM Enterprises did it, Stephanie Slate, director of talent acquisition for the multibillion-dollar automotive enterprise, said, "Our high associate engagement comes from a simple philosophy of two words: People First. This philosophy is embedded in our culture, and it's what really makes the difference."

Further, the company's turnover rate is just 7 percent, well below the industry average, which lowers expenses and improves profitability. It also means that the average tenure for employees is over ten years compared to the national average of 4.2 years. Due to the company's strong employer brand, most new hires come from referrals by current employees.

To top it off, JM Enterprises has had record revenues for the last five years, while maintaining annual growth of over 12 percent during the last seven years.

Top Tools to Attract, Hire, and Coach Winners

- **Identify your Top 5 customer-impacting jobs**—Create benchmarks for excellence for this group of employees. Build a hiring system that puts winners in these critical positions.

- **Create an exciting workplace**—People want to have fun on the job. They also want to learn, be challenged, and receive recognition for a job well done. If you don't provide these things, your best employees will find another company that does.

- **Pay attention to your employer brand**—Create a brand to attract employees to your business the same way you attract customers to your business. Have a similar budget, status, and directive. Savvy companies have their product brand managers become employer brand managers.

- **Be a different employer**—Companies like Zappos and Google have redefined the employee experience. But you don't have to be a billion-dollar company to create a culture that attracts the best candidates. Simply find ways to create an environment that offers fabulous fun, rewards, recognition, and personal convenience programs. How can you do this and stand out from the crowd?

- **Look for talent in nontraditional places**—Retirees, interns, college students, part-timers, parents at home, and independent contractors represent a rapidly increasing segment of the workforce. How are you engaging these kinds of employees?

- **Hire a full-time, on-staff recruiter**—Finding and hiring employees has become a full-time job for many companies. Recruit fifty-two weeks per year.

- **Improve your 8-Score**—Give people eight things in their jobs: compensation, recognition, fun, personal growth, challenge, convenience, security, and communication.

- **Become a student of recruiting**—Make a commitment to become an expert at recruiting. Brainstorm new approaches with different groups each month to see what other companies are doing, such as CEO peer groups, industry peer groups, chambers of commerce, and service clubs.

- **Hire consultants or independent contractors instead of employees**—Try putting experts like consultants on your board or in key roles. Many boards of directors/advisors work for almost no pay. A consultant might fill a role on a part-time basis for the same amount that a much less experienced full-time employee would.

- **Outsource everything**—Consider outsourcing functions that aren't your core business. They will almost always be more efficient and, therefore, more cost-effective. Ask yourself, "Why are we doing this? Aren't others better at it?"

For Further Thought

- What is your employer brand?
- How can you improve your employer brand?
- How can improve yourself and those around you at placing winners and coaching them?
- Jerry Goldress, the preeminent turnaround guru, talks about "putting winners in game-breaker positions." What are your game-breaker positions?
- How are you matching winners to the right positions?
- How frequent is coaching for your key people?
- Who is responsible for the hiring process in your company?

CEO Tools Case Study:

Teamwork Athletic Apparel, San Marcos, California

"I never intended to be in the family business," said Matt Lehrer, Teamwork Athletic Apparel's chief executive. "I had just finished applying to business school, and while I was trying to figure out the direction for my career, I decided to work for the family business for a month or two. I've been here ever since."

Teamwork Athletic Apparel is a leading manufacturer of team uniforms, outerwear, and fan wear for twelve of the world's sports. Established in 1987, this privately held, family-owned business has over 200 employees in San Marcos, California, and 150 employees in their satellite office in Mexico.

But when Matt Lehrer started, it was a small, eight-person company that sold athletic apparel to sports teams through local sports retailers, print shops, and promotional products companies. He bought the company from his parents in 1993 and grew it on the principle of fanatical execution. The company has survived through industry-threatening disruptions and today is one of America's largest and fastest-growing manufacturers and distributors of team athletic uniforms.

The first disruption hit when Chinese manufacturers flooded the market with low-cost jerseys, which they could produce at one-third Teamwork Athletic Apparel's cost. To battle this competitive pressure, Lehrer set up a manufacturing facility in Mexico, allowing his company to maintain better control of its processes and continue its focus on high-quality execution.

Ten years later there was another disruption. Retail and local specialty stores began to falter and even collapse under the onslaught of online shopping. Teamwork Athletic Apparel had to find another way to stay competitive in the fast-moving marketplace.

CEO Matt Lehrer heard about an innovative technology called *sublimation* that he thought they could apply, and it revolutionized their manufacturing process. The definition of *sublimation* is to change a solid to a gas, without passing through the liquid phase. In this process, a dye sublimation heat transfer printer uses heat to transfer the dye onto fabric without going through a liquid stage. The process completely changes the speed of the printing and complexity of the designs available.

This change gave Teamwork Athletic Apparel a tremendous advantage. Now all their inventory can be ordered in white. The colors are applied when the computer-generated design is applied to the fabric. Because of the way the dye bonds to the fabric, the colors produced are extraordinarily brilliant. The effect is even more dramatic because the process allows the image to be printed over the entire item, and it produces designs that are equivalent to photographic images. And anything that can be computer-designed can be applied.

The biggest advantage, however, is speed. With the new process, orders that had taken twenty-one days to fulfill could initially be completed in two to three days. Today, the company has shaved that time further to next-day or even same-day fulfillment on many products.

Set the Direction

Matt, his brother and partner, Andy, and their team set the direction for the company. The industry and its processes are changing so rapidly that they set an annual direction that is driven by quarterly objectives. This planning process allows for very agile deployment of new technologies and new opportunities while enabling the team to quickly address issues and implement solutions.

Communicate to Build Trust

Communication is paramount at Teamwork Athletic Apparel. The company values are displayed in every area of the sprawling facilities. They use the phrase "Catching the Culture Buzz" to describe how they get and keep everyone on the right track and aligned with how the company operates. The company has adopted a honeybee mascot to carry on the buzz theme, and posters in each area or department feature a honeycomb shape. One of the company's twelve values occupies each cell of the honeycomb.

These are the company's twelve values:

- **'Bee' Trustworthy**—Trust never goes out of style. We require honesty and integrity in everything we do. We do the right things for the right reasons.
- **'Bee' Self-Aware**—Don't put square pegs in round holes. We strive to place employees in jobs that are suited to their skills, knowledge, and unique abilities.
- **Above & Beyond**—Deliver above-and-beyond service. We differentiate ourselves by doing things that are above and beyond what's expected with regard to our service and striving to exceed the expectations of our customers, co-workers, and vendors.
- **'Bee' Respectful**—Maintain constructive relationships. We believe that no matter what happens, we should always respect everyone.
- **'Bee' Inventive**—Go where no one has gone before. We see obstacles as opportunities for us to overcome, showing us that we can achieve great things through innovation, creativity, and perseverance.
- **'Bee' Proactive**—See beyond today. We invest in our organization and people to ensure that, at all times, we are making the right strategic decisions to grow a thriving business now and far into the future.
- **'Bee' Positive**—Do something positive. We take the initiative to make things better with everything we do and are empowered to create solutions.
- **'Bee' Skilled**—Maintain your edge. We actively pursue education, skills development, and self-awareness, giving us the opportunity to achieve effective personal and professional growth.

- **'Bee' Better**—Take it to the next level. We are committed to continuous improvement and recognize our obligation to find new and better ways to improve our quality, efficiency, safety, and satisfaction to our customers on a daily basis.
- **'Bee' Responsible**—Be a responsible citizen. We believe in making a positive difference in the communities and environments that we live, work, and come in contact with. We build open and honest relationships with good communication.
- **'Bee' Collaborative**—Go team go. We value the power of bringing together talented individuals to form a team with energy, inspiration, unity, and a common bond that can accomplish things together.
- **'Bee' Unique**—Have fun! We have an environment that is diverse, friendly, and FUN!

Track Metrics and Give Feedback

To stay ahead in the company's uber-competitive marketplace, Teamwork Athletic Apparel is relentless about tracking metrics. Visual boards throughout the company show the progress on key metrics for the organization, the department, the team, or individual team members. These metrics provide information about past and current performance and, in some cases, project future needs and activities.

For example, charts posted in the call center use historical data to project upcoming call volumes, which are displayed on a board called the Call Alert Calendar. Being able to determine the projected activity by week and by individual shift allows the call center to staff appropriately. Further, the Call Alert Calendar builds awareness and a sense of responsibility within the team so that everyone is at work on time and prepared, especially when the call volume is projected to be heavy.

Anticipate the Future and Create It

Matt Lehrer and his team have responded to drastic marketplace shifts by constantly staying on top of issues as they arise, as well as anticipating issues before they arise. They know that it's critical to help their employees cope with and even embrace the pace of change.

When an organizational change is required, Teamwork Athletic Apparel uses a tool called VOTA to anticipate the future, establish a plan, and execute appropriate action. VOTA is a tool Matt learned from Dan Sullivan. Matt has been a longtime participant in Dan's program, "The Strategic Coach," which is designed to improve the results for high-performing executives and entrepreneurs.

VOTA is an acronym:

V = The vision plans for what needs to be done

O = Obstacles that may block implementation

T = Transformation needed to complete plans

A = Actions needed to create the needed change

Here's why this process is so important. Visions can be set for all types of outcomes. In most cases, once goals are set, the mind tends to drift to the obstacles that might be encountered when attempting to meet the goal or vision. When facing obstacles, there's a natural tendency to get stuck and become to immobilized or indecisive about what to do. This is often referred to as *analysis paralysis*.

When people need to make a key decision, they want to feel confident. Matt says this actually takes more courage than confidence.

"The truth is that having courage feels crappy at the time," he shared, "because it requires you to take action in the face of fear or doubt." It doesn't feel like confidence until you move into action.

The VOTA process can be used to establish and accomplish a big-picture, long-term goal or to take one minute for a routine task that must be fit into a busy schedule.

Attract, Hire, and Coach Winners

Teamwork Athletic Apparel believes in growing the business by growing its people. The company is committed to getting winners on its team and believes that good people can have three times the impact of average people—and that *great* people can have three times the impact of good people.

The company uses nontraditional interviewing techniques to ensure they attract great people. Having employed over 10,000 people during the last decade, the company is getting great results from the tool *Make Them Do It*.

For example, when they hire for a key customer-impacting position in the customer service department, the final candidate fields a call from a "customer," who is actually one of the hiring team members. In the early days that even included the CEO, Matt Lehrer. Lehrer designed a process where the hiring team member doesn't see the candidate, a picture of the candidate, or a resume for the candidate, or even know the candidate's name. It's an attempt to eliminate or limit any cognitive bias.

The interviewer gives the prospective employee a scenario that describes a particular product and process, and then the prospect fields a call from the "customer," not knowing it's a hiring team member. During the call, the candidate is asked for things that cannot be delivered. The sole purpose of this exercise is to find out how they would handle this difficult situation.

Apparently, this method works because the customer service team has won numerous Stevie Awards, beating out giants in the service field like LL Bean, Amazon, and Nordstrom.

Teamwork Athletic Apparel also adopted this process for other areas of the business and for manager candidates to ensure that the candidate's response aligns with the company's business values.

Create an Autonomous Organization

Teamwork Athletic Apparel reinforces its directions and values using regularly held meetings, including company-wide town hall meetings, small group meetings, and brown bag lunch meetings.

As a longtime member of YPO (formerly Young Presidents' Organization), Matt Lehrer receives ongoing feedback from other successful young executives who share their successes and challenges in the spirit of mutual learning and growth.

He has always been adamant about building the team's talent from within the organization. Most recently, he showed confidence in the team by assuming the role of chairman and turning over day-to-day operations to the company's president.

Celebrate Successes

The fact that the company celebrates successes and gives recognition to employees is evident when walking in the door at Teamwork Athletic Apparel. The receptionist's nameplate reads "The Director of First Impressions." Behind her, a video taken at a recent company-wide town hall meeting plays.

In the video, employees are playing games, listening to music, and enjoying food and refreshments. Their smiling faces show that they are having fun—in the company parking lot that was decorated to resemble a fair or carnival. At that meeting, Matt and his team presented company news, acknowledged birthdays and anniversaries, and shared departmental and individual accomplishments.

Teamwork Athletic Apparel also has a peer recognition program that ties into the company values boards with the honeycomb. Employees can fill out a card that recognizes another employee and place it on the value that the colleague exemplified. The boards in some of the departments are covered with these tributes.

Chapter Six

Build an Autonomous Company

The CEO Tools Business System

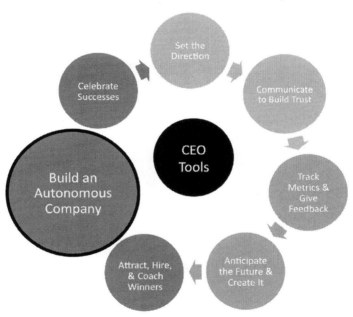

COMMUNICATE • EXECUTE • OPTIMIZE

Eighty-five percent of the reasons for failure are deficiencies in systems and process rather than the employee. The role of management should be to change the process rather than badgering the people to do better.

—W. Edward Deming

Jack was making great time today. He was averaging under eight minutes a mile, which would be a personal record if he could maintain it. The sun reflected over the still waters of the lake as he pushed hard up the last hill. On reaching the top, he looked at his watch. He'd done it! He'd finished the three-mile run in just under twenty-five minutes.

"You're looking quite fit, Jack," his friend called out. "Better than ever!"

Jack could barely contain himself. "I'm in the best shape I've been in since college, and the company is running really well. We followed your model and hired two new managers from the outside and promoted one from within. It's invigorated not only the team, but the whole organization. It's like they can sense the new energy these key hires have brought to the company.

"The whole team is committed to ongoing coaching for our employees, and, although we've had to part ways with a couple of people, the majority have responded really well. Their performance and attitudes aren't only improving, they're contagious."

Jack's friend nodded in approval. "You're on your way! Your company is growing, profitable, and easier to manage, and it has the potential to give you the freedom and flexibility to live the way you want. May I ask a couple of questions?"

Jack chuckled at the question—the one that used to give him cold chills. "Fire away!" he said confidently.

"Things are running great with you at the helm. But would it run as smoothly if you weren't at the center of things all the time?"

Jack's first thought was to say that if something happened to him, his team would rally around the company and keep things running. Then he thought about a different situation. What if he was on vacation, traveling the world? Would people know what to do in his absence?

"I don't know," he said. "At least I'm not sure."

"I've got some thoughts on how you can ensure ongoing performance, if you have time."

Jack smiled and nodded that he had time.

"What it comes down to is that people have to understand their roles, their responsibilities, and the rules in order to perform without your specific guidance, input, or decisions. They have to be able to rely on each other and on the processes to give them the guidance they need. It's more than knowing their own jobs. They have to understand who's responsible

for everything that's critical to the company's success, even when those things aren't necessarily assigned to a specific person."

He could see that Jack was listening attentively but didn't fully grasp what he was saying.

"Let me give you some examples. We know who's responsible for making decisions about marketing. It's the chief marketing officer, or CMO. But what about the company's values? Who is your CVO, your chief values officer? Or what about quality? Who is the CQO, your chief quality officer? And who is in charge of recognition and making things fun?"

Jack continued to listen, and he learned some other ways he could organize the business to sustain performance without him.

In hundreds of meetings with company leaders—chief executives, presidents, and owners—I've asked, "What would you like more of from your company?"

There were three predominant answers:

- Better profits with improved margins and better cash flows

- Easier, more reliable execution of strategic objectives

- More time with family and friends and for personal travel

Now, take a look at the facts:

- According to the Wells Fargo/Gallup Small Business Index, the average small business owner works more than fifty hours per week, and almost 60 percent report working six days a week. And more than 20 percent work *seven* days a week.

- About 85 percent of business owners surveyed reported that they had to be on site daily because they were the primary person responsible for core functions like production or service, managing the day-to-day business, and managing the financial aspects of the business.

What could be driving this? It's the old hub-and-spoke syndrome, where the chief executive (maybe even the whole senior team) is the hub, and the spokes must be connected to get anything done. If you want to create an autonomous company, it must be able to succeed and grow without you at the center of all activities. Your employees should be more than spokes that connect to you.

Business leaders are often reluctant to give up this central position because they like to serve their customers personally. It feels good to solve problems. Happy customers shower you with praise, you feel needed, and you know your customers are getting the best care from your very own hands. After all, you know your business better than anybody, and training others to do the job takes a lot of time and can cost a lot of money.

But here's the truth of the matter: the more your customers need you and want you personally, the harder it is for you to focus on what you should be doing—growing your business.

What Is an Autonomous Organization?

Building an autonomous company means the *organization* and its *processes* must be the center hub, rather than a person. Remember management guru Peter Drucker's words: "The bottleneck is always at the top of the bottle."

Keith McFarland, author of *The Breakthrough Company,* studied the companies that made the *Inc.* 1000 list over a ten-year period. He looked at which ones had created a breakthrough by growing to greater than $100 million in revenue while maintaining their profitability and independent ownership. Then he looked for similarities in how these companies achieved that growth. One thing they had in common is what he calls "crowning the company."

Crowning the company means putting the company and its processes first. You lean on and leverage the power of ordinary people to do extraordinary things by refining and optimizing the processes that drive results.

McFarland describes the four stages of moving out of the hub-and-spoke model and building an autonomous organization:

- One-man band

- Tribal clan

- Village elders

- Sovereign organization

The *one-man band* describes an organization where the owners and managers are directly responsible for delivering all the technical aspects of the business, and they handle all aspects of running the business.

Next, organizations move into the *tribal clan* phase where managers begin to delegate responsibility and coach people to perform. As the company grows more sophisticated in its management, delegation, and coaching, the business moves to the *village elder* phase.

If the company leaders can transition to a strategic and coaching role, the business transcends to the *sovereign organization*—what we call the autonomous company in *CEO Tools* language. In this model, the leaders move from an autocratic approach of commanding and controlling to an autonomous approach of coaching and encouraging.

In autocratic organizations, the people at the top make the decisions. The chief executive and other senior team members become the backstop for all requests, questions, resource allocations, decisions, and problem-solving. Middle managers handle routine day-to-day tasks, like scheduling and performance management, but their people make few decisions and simply follow directions to deliver output.

In autonomous organizations, by contrast, the senior team focuses on fewer—and therefore more critical—decisions. McKinsey & Co. calls these "big-bet decisions." These are decisions that have major consequences for the company but often involve situations where right or wrong solutions are unclear. The executives set the initial levels of delegation and work interdependently to develop the processes that provide the backbone for their autonomous culture.

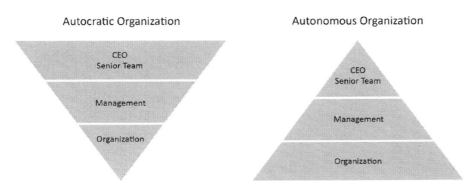

Autocratic Organization	Autonomous Organization
CEO Senior Team	CEO Senior Team
Management	Management
Organization	Organization

In the autonomous model, middle managers manage *processes first* and *people second*. If an issue arises, they look for a root cause in the process before admonishing people. The organization is now engaged in execution and decision-making within the delegated framework and the established processes. There is ongoing focus to make incremental improvements in the process to enhance results. It's presumed that the people doing the work often have the best ideas about how to improve the processes.

• • •

Delegating decision-making and ongoing process improvement is what has made Danaher Corporation so successful. The corporation's more than twenty-five operating companies generate almost $20 billion in total revenues, while significantly outperforming the S&P 500 for over twenty years.

Danaher calls its approach the Danaher Business System (DBS). According to the company's own description, the DBS is fueled by the corporation's core values, which drive the company through a never-ending cycle of change and improvement: exceptional *people* develop outstanding *plans* and execute them using world-class tools to construct sustainable *processes*, resulting in superior *performance*. Danaher's employer brand attracts exceptional people who continue the cycle by their commitment to the organization's four customer-facing priorities: quality, delivery, cost, and innovation.

• • •

Autonomous organizations must be sustainable, which means that the systems and processes continue and are maintained over time. A sustainable process must have the capacity to absorb disturbances and still retain its structure and ability to deliver results. It must be able to deliver the long-term vision while being responsive to immediate events.

Creating an Autonomous Business Model

To create an autonomous business model, the seven basic processes shown below must be considered, identified, and tracked.

Processes to Optimize Autonomy

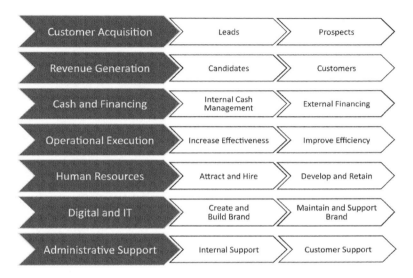

Customer Acquisition	Leads	Prospects
Revenue Generation	Candidates	Customers
Cash and Financing	Internal Cash Management	External Financing
Operational Execution	Increase Effectiveness	Improve Efficiency
Human Resources	Attract and Hire	Develop and Retain
Digital and IT	Create and Build Brand	Maintain and Support Brand
Administrative Support	Internal Support	Customer Support

Seven Fundamental Business Processes

Customer Acquisition Process. In the customer acquisition process, the company determines how it will attract leads and prospects. Leads are people or companies that have the potential to do business with you. Prospects are people or companies that have indicated an interest in doing business with you. In other words, prospects are leads who have responded in some way to your requests for engagement and action. Mature organizations that have become stagnant or plateaued have often lost the will or ability to generate new prospective customers on a consistent and reliable basis.

Revenue-Generation Process. In the revenue-generation process, leads and prospects are converted into candidates and customers. Candidates have put themselves in a decision-making position and will either choose your offering or an alternative; or they are deciding between several options you have offered them. This decision point is sometimes referred to as FMOT—the first moment of truth—when the buying decision is made at a website, a retail shelf, or through acceptance of a proposal. Every successful company must have a reliable and predictable process to convert prospects into customers and, in turn, generate revenue.

Cash and Financing Process. When a prospect has said "yes" to the offer and is ready to do business, sales convert to cash. The cash and financing process evaluates how sales convert to cash to meet the current and future cash needs of the organization, so it can meet its financial obligations and make capital investments. This process considers the amount of cash that can be generated to meet the current obligations based on current sales volume, margin, and costs. It also considers and anticipates the need for outside financing or investment, and matches that need with appropriate resources.

Operational Execution Process. The operational execution process focuses on making, delivering, or producing the product or service that generates the revenue. It involves planning, organizing, coordinating, and controlling all the resources needed.

Managing operations involves managing people, equipment, technology, information, and all the other resources needed in the production of goods and services. Operations processes are at the center of the other processes of every company. This applies to companies of all sizes and industries, and to manufacturing, distribution, and service companies. It applies as well to both for-profit and not-for-profit enterprises.

Human Resources Process. The human resources process is focused on attracting and hiring great people and then developing and retaining them. The administrative functions typically involve payroll, benefits, and conflict resolution. The HR unit also plays a key role in instilling the values and culture in the organization and provides ongoing learning and development opportunities to improve employee performance and cultivate future leaders.

Digital and Information Technology Process. The digital and information technology process is an ever-evolving part of any business. In years past, this process was focused on what hardware the company should invest in; more recently, the focus has turned to the software needed to run the business. With the introduction and subsequent reliance on the Web, these processes came to include websites, software-as-a-service, and e-commerce.

The digital and information technology process is also responsible for creating and building the brand presence online and then maintaining and supporting the brand through data acquisition, website development, and social media platforms. This process sorts out how the brands will follow two strategies: (1) the tell, talk, teach, or train processes; and (2) the sell, show, source, and search processes.

Tell, talk, teach, or train processes inform and communicate, and they apply internally and externally. Internally, this process specifies how to communicate your brand vision and promises, and it provides a platform to teach and train your people. Externally, you must assist customers with new or different uses for products and services.

Sell, show, source, and search processes help prospects and customers find, understand, and choose the products or services that meet their needs.

Administrative Support Process. Administrative support covers both internal and external support processes. Internal support may include traditional administrative support of individuals or departments through clerical support, calendar scheduling and management, correspondence and reports, meetings coordination, and travel arrangements. It can also include maintaining a front desk or phone switchboard. Larger organizations may provide support in the form of legal or purchasing.

Externally focused administrative support processes include customer service and technical support and, in public companies, regulatory and shareholder support.

Optimizing the Processes

To optimize these processes, focus first on increasing the *effectiveness* of making, delivering, or producing your product or service. After that, you can refine and improve the *efficiencies* of making, delivering, or producing the product or service to maximize margin and volume.

Too often companies get that backwards. They find a problem with margin or profit and try to improve efficiencies to cut costs. This can easily backfire because it can stress a system that doesn't operate effectively. Sometimes you have to slow down to speed up. *Effectiveness* is about doing the right task, completing activities, and achieving goals. *Efficiency* is about doing things in the best possible way, which might include doing it faster or with fewer resources.

Process Improvement

Every time you go through the same steps to create an outcome, you're creating a process—whether it's to generate a report, resolve a customer complaint, contact a new client, or manufacture a product.

Ineffective or inefficient processes cause a number of issues and problems. Unhappy or dissatisfied customers, missed deadlines, increased costs, and overall organizational stress are just some of the results of dysfunctional processes.

Start by documenting your current processes in a systems handbook or standard operating procedures handbook. This is known as *mapping a process*. There are many ways to do process mapping, and the goal is to understand how a process works from beginning to end, using anything from simple flowcharts to complex diagrams and models. A favorite is a very visual diagram created by Kaoru Ishakawa in the late 1960s and known as a fishbone diagram.

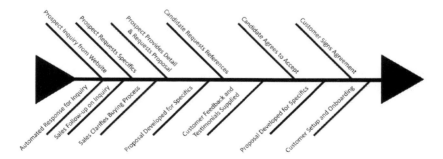

In this example, we're mapping how a customer is acquired. Start with a timeline that extends from the beginning of the process to the end of the process. Next, we'll add diagonal lines to the top of the timeline to indicate activities that customers do, in chronological sequence, and to the bottom of the timeline to indicate the company's activities along the timeline. It's like ping-pong: they do something, you do something, they do something, you do something, they do something, you do something, and so on. It becomes obvious why this is called a fishbone diagram.

This method allows you to examine the process and ask a series of questions:

- Where is our process strongest?

- Where is the process weakest, causing us to lose customers?

- Where do we need to add new resources?

- What parts no longer add value and can be eliminated or reduced?

- How can we improve the desired outcome by changing the process?

When a problem area is identified, you can combine another technique—the 5 Whys—to identify the root cause of the problem. Here's a simple example showing how to use the 5 Whys.

Problem: Customer refuses to pay for a print job for flyers

- Why? Order was not delivered on time and could not be used. (1st why)
- Why? Job took longer than expected and scheduled. (2nd why)
- Why? Ran out of ink. (3rd why)
- Why? Ink was used on a large, last-minute order. (4th why)
- Why? Not enough ink on hand and unable to secure more in time. (5th why, the root cause)

In this example, either finding an ink supplier who can deliver on short notice or increasing the minimum inventory of ink on hand will prevent similar problems from occurring in the future.

Delegate and Communicate to Build an Autonomous Company

For your organization to operate autonomously, you must do two things well: delegate and communicate.

Delegate Down to the Lowest Level

Leaders often struggle to delegate, for good reason. You probably think you can do the job best if you do it yourself—and that's probably true, at least initially. But if you never take time to train and coach others, you'll become a bottleneck preventing your team members from developing the skills needed to increase their value to the organization. Yes, it will take longer the first time someone else does it; and yes, that employee probably won't do it as well as you could. But over time, you'll actually give yourself the gift of time, because someone else will be providing that service and value.

Another reason that leaders have trouble letting go is they think that delegation is an all-or-nothing activity, like turning a switch on or off. We either do it all ourselves, or we hand it over completely to someone else. But delegating is actually more like a *dimmer switch*. Think in terms of levels of delegation that gradually get turned up:

- **Level 1**—I do it all: I seek alternatives (task 1), evaluate options (task 2), make a choice (task 3), and execute the choice (task 4).

- **Level 2**—I do the four Level 1 tasks while training someone else to be responsible for the decision in the future.

- **Level 3**—The employee performs task 1; I perform tasks 2-4.

- **Level 4**—The employee performs tasks 1-2 and makes a recommendation for task 3; I evaluate the task 3 recommendation and perform task 4.

- **Level 5**—The employee performs tasks 1-4 and reports the results to me.

This model allows you to *incrementally transfer* your knowledge and processes in a way that matches your employee's knowledge, skill, and experience. It also allows you to speak clearly about delegation in terms of understandable levels. As you move through the levels with an employee, you can ask, "Are you ready for Level 5 delegation on this activity?" By posing this question, you ensure that you and the employee agree on the expectations.

To create and maintain an autonomous company that can grow and thrive, you must push decision-making down to the *lowest possible level* in the company. To determine the appropriate place in the organization, consider experience and frequency. Authorize employees with the most experience with the situation to make the decision, and you'll get faster, better, more well-executed decisions while fostering stronger engagement at every level of the company.

For hiring, purchasing, production, and scheduling decisions, for example, employees who are closest to the process are the most *invested* in the outcome. They'll not only understand what's needed to make the decision, they'll also live with the results.

Decisions that are made infrequently but that will have a big impact usually call for people with a unique background and experience who can fully analyze the problem and execute the solution. These are the "big strategic bets" that Keith McFarland describes in *The Breakthrough Company*, requiring the senior team and very likely outside advisers to consider the strategic implications for the company before a decision is made.

To realign decision-making in your company so decisions are made at the most appropriate level, ask each manager, team, or department to make a list of the fifteen to twenty most frequently made decisions. Consider each one and discuss the following:

- Is the decision easy to reverse?
- Is the proposed person capable of making the decision?
- Is tracking in place to create accountability for the results of the decision?

If the answer to all three questions is "yes," then delegate the decision to the proposed individual. Senior team members should only make decisions that are hard to reverse, that require their specific capabilities, or that are difficult to track.

Finally, establish a protocol to escalate a decision when it's necessary. Define who the decision maker should report to if a situation is too pressing or significant to permit normal practices.

> Amazon and Toyota both implemented a concept known as *Andon*. This Japanese word means *light* or *lantern*, and it signifies a show-stopping, immediate action to arrest a problem.
>
> At Amazon, chief executive Jeff Bezos refers to the customer service Andon pull cord, a metaphorical cord an employee is told to pull if any situation will reduce the value a customer receives because of Amazon's pricing or practices.
>
> At Saturn's manufacturing plant in Tennessee, line workers were instructed to pull a red handle to stop the assembly line if they identified a defect that, if not resolved, would move down the line or be repeated.

Communicate Frequently, Transparently, and Authentically

You've probably noticed that communication is part of almost every chapter in *CEO Tools 2.0*. This is both by design and at the request of every stakeholder in your company: employees, managers, customers, vendors, and shareholders. Each stakeholder has the same need for the company to communicate *more frequently* with *greater* transparency in *authentic* language. Think about how to *overcommunicate* rather than communicate, and you'll probably hit the right mark.

It's important to create a scheduled and structured communication process to keep people informed about routine decisions, upcoming changes, and achievements. The goal is to eliminate the I-didn't-know phenomenon, which derails delegation and decision-making efforts, and creates a victim mentality and learned helplessness.

Ensuring that everyone is on the same page is one of the benefits of a twelve-month company calendar—perhaps one of the most useful and effective communication tools you can create. It's a great way to ensure that your entire team stays on top of meetings, the dates of important deliverables, visits by off-site employees or consultants, and other company business and events.

A company calendar accomplishes two more things. It tells employees that you trust them to manage their own time and hit the due dates on the calendar. And the clarity that the calendar provides allows employees to plan their vacations months ahead without fear that a company obligation will sabotage their plans. It's a win-win-win—for you, for your team members, and for the company.

As you think about other communications, consider the value of creating a communications *schedule* for your company. Remember, your goal should be to *overcommunicate* to your team.

To help you get started, here's a suggestion for annual, quarterly, monthly, weekly, and daily communications:

Annually—Set the company direction.

- Debrief and review the prior year's results. Focus on the facts and metrics, not the stories, to determine what actually happened.

- Using your analysis, update the multiyear strategic plans and develop the current year's annual tactics to establish next actions and quarterly objectives.

- Review resource allocations and determine what, if any, capital investments should be made for the future of the company.

- Create a budget for the upcoming year.

- Engage your people in these conversations. Solicit their opinions, and challenge them to come up with new and fresh approaches.

- Communicate the results of these activities using the One-Page Business Plan and through a full complement of communication tools—written, visual, and verbal—in small groups, company meetings, and one-on-one.

Quarterly

- Review the actual results versus projected results using the Quarterly Priorities Manager (QPM) and Quarterly Debrief. The Quarterly Debrief follows a structured format. Ask what went well. Once the successes and accomplishments have been gathered, ask, "Can we expect more of that?"

- Review what didn't work for the quarter. Watch for justifications and deflecting responsibility. Create an atmosphere of blameless problem-solving. Ask, "What did we learn from what happened?" The answers can prevent you from repeating the situation or realizing the same outcome. If the conversation about what was learned wasn't very positive, turn that around by asking, "Who should we appreciate for their contribution? Who made a difference, created a great result, or pitched in across departments to help out?"

- Then ask how they should be recognized and by whom. (Chapter seven provides many ideas about how to recognize people.) Obviously, the kudos should come from their manager or supervisor, but sometimes you can make a bigger impact if the recognition comes from someone else in the company—for example, the chief executive officer or the head of another department.

- Conduct quarterly business reviews with the whole company. Often called "all-hands meetings," they have formal agendas but a casual feel. Include a financial review, market growth and penetration review, new customer acquisition highlights, and an operations and service/support report. And be sure to recognize newly hired people, employees celebrating work anniversaries, and any other significant events.

Monthly

- Each month, review results and make any needed course corrections. Use the metrics on Trailing 12 Month (T12M) Charts and look for opportunities for recognition.

- Engage direct reports in one-on-one meetings to continue building those relationships and to build trust.

Weekly

- Review results weekly to identify any issues and assess cash needs. Weekly reviews serve as an early-warning system, eliminating surprises that could otherwise come too late in the month to rectify.

- Avoid the need for last-minute pushes for orders or sales by identifying any shortfalls during the first and second weeks of the month.

Daily

- Some companies or departments benefit from a daily huddle—a short stand-up meeting or a conference call to establish quick priorities and address any issues.

- Every day, walk the four corners, and check in on your key players to see if you can help them or support their efforts.

• • •

Ken Hazen, chief executive at CTSI, a freight payment and logistics company in Memphis, Tennessee, learned the value of asking, "Can we expect more?" Working toward an annual goal of $10 million in revenue, his team was giddy to report in a meeting that quarterly revenues would come in well above the $2.5 million target. But when Hazen asked the group, "Can we expect more?" the room grew quiet.

"Actually," one team member shared, "our numbers for this quarter include some business that we originally projected for next quarter. So although we're on target for this quarter, we're now behind for next quarter."

With this new clarity on the company's revenue picture, instead of heading out early to celebrate, the team developed a strategy for making up the shortfall in the next quarter, so they could stay on track to meet the annual goal.

• • •

Chip Conley, founder and former chief executive of JDV Hotels, the second-largest boutique hotel chain in the United States, tells a story to illustrate how important recognition can be when it comes from outside a high-performing employee's department.

On a busy holiday weekend, the only elevator at a renovated period property near Union Square in San Francisco went out of service. A dedicated bellman who'd planned to spend the holiday with his visiting family canceled his time off and worked twelve-hour shifts to make sure that arriving guests' bags were hand-carried up the narrow stairs and delivered to their rooms.

When the management team heard the story, the head of IT offered to be the one to personally recognize the bellman. He could relate to that kind of effort, he said, because his team often had to abandon personal plans to deal with technology issues that occurred late at night or on weekends.

Being recognized by the head of IT made a big difference to the bellman and reinforced his already strong commitment to the company.

Lead, Manage, Do

Once you successfully delegate, you'll be in the enviable position of being able to choose how to best use your time. Where you decide to spend your time can have make-or-break effects on your company, so you'll want to make these decisions carefully and thoughtfully.

One approach to determining your time allocation is to break your time into three broad categories: leading, managing, and doing. Think about how much time you now invest in each category. Then look to the future, and consider how much time you'd like to spend in each category.

If you have no real sense of how you now spend your time, consider tracking your time at the end of every day for one or two weeks. For each day, write down the number of hours you spent leading, managing, and doing. You may find the results surprising. But regardless, you'll have a solid starting point based on reality.

Effective leaders generally spend their time as shown in this table:

	Chief Executive/ President	Managers
Leading	45-60%	25-40%
Managing and Coaching	20-35%	35-45%
Doing	10-20%	20-30%

Here are some tools for use in each category of activity:

Leading	W4C	Monthly Letter	Recognition Tools
Managing and Coaching	QPM	One-on-One	T12M
Doing	Time Audit	Company Calendar	"A" Activities

It's also important to step back and look at the bigger picture. Try this visualization tool, which helps you go from ground level to 30,000 feet for thirty minutes. From 30,000 feet, look down and observe what you see. Take in the company, the industry, your competitors, your customers. What do you see from this vantage point?

This big-picture thinking takes you into the realm of giants because it separates your thoughts about what is possible from your everyday thoughts about what is probable.

Along the same lines, Dr. Tom Hill, an internationally known business leader, speaker, and author of *Living at the Summit* and other books, recommends a personal retreat. He suggests going off by yourself once a year to a relaxing, secluded spot where you can just sit and think. It could be a mountain, a sandy beach, or even a favorite bench at a local park—anywhere you can spend time alone to think without distractions. Determine how to best invest your time, think about big ideas for the business, and refocus on what's important in your future.

Our entrepreneurial natures can cause us to be so fully immersed in our businesses that, regardless of how we plan to allocate our time among the various areas, we still spend nearly 100 percent of our time on the job. It can occupy our every waking moment, plus much of our dream time. For our own sanity as well as the health of the business, we need to buy back some time for our family, for our friends, and for ourselves.

Roles-at-the-Top Exercise

What would you say is the most important aspect of your business? Usually things like customer satisfaction, revenue and profit growth, company values, and employee satisfaction come to mind. Next, look at how your organization is structured. You probably have a chief executive officer, a chief operations executive, and a chief financial executive, among others.

You may find, however, that some of the things that are critical to your success don't have a specific person in charge of them. They need a champion.

In the following exercise, you'll divide these important things among your executives and managers to assign a champion who will track and manage the outcomes. In this exercise, the chief executive and senior managers assign a champion but trade roles from one area to another area periodically to help, align, fix, support, and ensure success for the long term.

The following list of roles might help illuminate this concept. Identify the individual who is monitoring these things in your company.

TITLE	KEY RESULT	WHO IS WATCHING
CCO	Customer	_____
CSRO	Sales/Revenue	_____
CSO	Strategy	_____
CVO	Vision	_____
CPO	Planning	_____
CTO	Technology	_____
CQO	Quality	_____
CFO	Financial	_____
CGO	Goals	_____
CMTO	Metric Tracking	_____
CGRO	Growth	_____
CULO	Culture	_____
CVO	Values	_____
CCMO	Communication	_____
CRO	Recognition	_____
CPO	Passion	_____
CFUNO	Fun!	_____
CHRO	People	_____
CAO	Administrative	_____

The answer to the question, "Who is monitoring these areas?" often is either "everyone" or "me." If *everyone* is keeping tabs on something, that usually means that *nobody* is, because each person thinks someone else watching it. And if the answer to that question is *me*, then that means no one's watching it as well, since no single leader can keep up with all those areas at once.

Gather your managers together to rate the current performance in these key areas on a one-to-ten scale. A score of one is terrible; something must be done immediately. A score of 10 is great, or almost perfect.

Compile the results to determine which areas need the most attention. Ask the group to brainstorm ideas to address weaker areas. This exercise can yield remarkable results, because your people always know where the weak spots are—and they know how to fix them. The problem is, they usually don't have the time, the teamwork, or all the tools to fix them.

The Roles-at-the-Top exercise is about setting goals for each key area and divvying up the responsibility for getting them done. Try meeting once a month to challenge each other on the progress. Check off the action items and form some new ones. Coach and help each other to reassess on a continuing basis. Then rotate the non-job-specific roles at least annually.

Ronnie Randall was a world-class owner and former chief executive of Kele Company in Memphis, Tennessee, a great example of an autonomous company. Randall changed his title to chief culture officer and made safeguarding the company culture his area of responsibility.

If you visited the Kele offices, you'd invariably pass a team working on process improvement and a group in a learning session. You'd also notice messaging and scoreboards throughout the building to remind people about what was important and meaningful.

Randall said his job was to create, monitor, and maintain a company culture that he was proud of. If he did that, he believed, the results would follow. And that's what happened, to the tune of almost $100 million in revenues.

Top Tools to Build an Autonomous Company

- **Manage and improve processes**—Identify, record, and document the processes in key business areas. Use process mapping tools to identify opportunities to improve processes to conserve resources and add value. Commit to ongoing process improvement.

- **Delegate decision-making**—Move decision-making closer to those who will implement the decision. Specify the level of delegation when tasks and decisions are handed over to someone else.

- **Create roles at the top**—Set roles to focus on what is important in your business each year, and put champions in charge of taking care of customers, growth, profit, and people. Who are your VPs of customer satisfaction, growth, profit, and fun?

- **Utilize the Quarterly Priorities Manager**—Introduced in chapter two, the QPM resurfaces here to encourage managers to share five individual quarterly goals with each other on a regular basis and then help each other achieve them.

- **Create a twelve-month company calendar**—Share all key events with all your employees to create coordinated results. Each quarter, the months that just ended are appended for the next year, creating a perpetual calendar.

- **Utilize quarterly and monthly business reviews**—QBRs are the perfect vehicle for applying tracking tools and anticipating the future. Turbo-charge your actions as a leader and manager.

- **Commit to lifelong learning**—Join a peer group for leaders. Memberships in groups that assemble leaders to exchange experiences and ideas are successful in improving businesses and enhancing the lives of members.

- **Develop a meeting cadence**—Develop a reliable schedule for annual, quarterly, monthly, and weekly meetings. Make the meetings interesting, informative, and, whenever possible, fun.

- **Hold daily fifteen-minute meetings**—Ritz-Carlton hotels probably invented this concept with their ten-minute stand-up review of what's important in guest service. Your daily fifteen-minute stand-up meetings could review the previous day's lessons and today's improvements with your key managers and players.

For Further Reflection

- How effective are your company's key business processes?
- Can they be learned and accomplished by others, or are they overly reliant on a key person?
- What process improvement tools do you use?
- How are you creating ongoing improvement in your key processes?
- When did you last map the value stream for your processes?

CEO Tools Case Study:
Total Transit, Inc., Phoenix, Arizona

The way Craig C. Hughes, founder and chairman of Total Transit, Inc., tells it, he got into the wrong business in the wrong industry at the wrong time—with no industry experience. Not exactly a recipe for success!

In 1984, with his wife, Chris, Hughes bought an airport cab company with fifteen cars and promptly lost $20,000 in the first few months. Struggling to recoup their losses, the couple created a dispatch cab company and named it Discount Cab Company. Today, Discount Cab is recognized throughout the country as an industry leader, thanks to its ability to deliver high-value services via the effective use of innovative and progressive solutions.

Total Transit, Inc. is the holding entity for several lines of business. In addition to Discount Cab, a public transportation division provides services for private and public entities, including transit authorities. They rolled the transportation management company into their original tech company and created a new company, Veyo, a next-generation medical logistics technology company.

Veyo—which provides reliable, affordable transportation to medical appointments for millions of Medicaid beneficiaries—is revolutionizing nonemergency medical transportation with a technology-first approach to patient transportation. Using real-time dashboards, supply-and-demand analytics, and passenger and driver apps, the GPS-tracking and predictive analytics allow Veyo cars to be available when and where they're needed.

Hughes and his team also created a platform that utilizes drivers who use their own vehicles, much like Uber and Lyft.

Total Transit, Inc. generates over $250 million in annual revenues across all platforms, with over 500 employees and thousands more independent contractors. Hughes tells his story in *The Self-Driving Company: How Getting Out of the Way Enabled My Company to Thrive*. Total Transit is now an autonomous organization, and here's how Hughes and his team did it.

Set the Direction

Total Transit's strategic planning process is part of the company's DNA. The strategic plan includes four elements:

- **Vision**—Identifying the company's long-term direction
- **Mission**—Defining the company's purpose
- **Core principles**—Providing the company's decision-making foundation
- **Strategy**—Articulating what the company will do, where it will do it, and how it will win

"We want the strategic plan to be a document that causes action, not one that sits on a shelf," says Mike Pinckard, chief executive officer.

Total Transit, Inc. is a values-driven company, and these core principles drive its culture:

- Operate transparently with honesty and integrity
- Manage risk and the impact on the environment
- Attract, mentor, and retain the best people
- Understand customer needs and exceed expectations
- Be an indispensable member of the community
- Encourage innovation and embrace change

Communicate to Build Trust

The company's leaders believe the best way to build trust is to give trust, so they give their people the responsibility to act on their own judgment. They spend more time training their people on their core principles and the fundamentals of decision-making than on the processes themselves. This approach allows decisions to be made on the front line, in real time, for increased customer satisfaction.

Track Metrics and Give Feedback

Measuring metrics is important, but measuring the *right metrics* is critical. Pinckard learned this in his first days with the company.

Right from the start, something puzzled him. He was sitting in his office when he heard a bell ring. Then he heard it ring again. After hearing the bell five or six more times, he asked why. The company's practice was to ring a bell every time a new contract was signed. *Great,* Pinckard thought. *Lots of bells must mean lots of new business.*

Pinckard was thrilled—until he looked at the financial statements. The P&L showed no revenue growth. A little digging revealed that signed contracts didn't convert to revenue until they generated trips, and that could be awhile—or never. But that wasn't all. The sales team was comped on signed contracts, not revenue.

Lessons learned. Now the company's metrics measure *real* results, and its comp packages mirror *real* outcomes.

Every Total Transit department has its own dashboard. The call center, leasing department, and business development unit each track metrics that relate to better managing their particular daily activities.

In the early days of the company, the taxi industry generally wasn't good at matching demand for service with vehicle availability. So Total Transit developed a forecasting system that accurately forecasted trip volumes by the hour of the day and the day of the week. This ability to align supply and demand contributed to average annual growth of over 20 percent, even during difficult economic cycles.

Anticipate the Future and Create It

Hughes took his What's Next? planning to heart. A devoted follower of Tom Hill, author of *Living at the Summit*, Hughes used Hill's direction to approach life in eighteen-month segments to create meaningful change.

In 2008, he looked ahead four eighteen-month cycles to envision his perfect life six years out. Sequestering himself, he sought the answer to a big question: What would make up his perfect life? He wrote down what he pictured in detail: the sounds, the smells, and the sights he'd experience if his perfect life materialized.

Hughes was so energized by this exercise that he shared what he'd written with his management team at the next planning session. He pictured the $20 million company, the biggest cab company in Phoenix, as a $100+ million company in six years, meaning that annual growth would have to exceed 35 percent. He saw that each of the five people on the management team would be a millionaire. Top-notch presidents would head each operating division, and the company would take 12,000 calls each day and dispatch 1,000 cabs. By 2020, he told the team, Total Transit would be a $1 billion company. Now, that's a big, audacious goal!

Hughes's dream for the company excited the team, and every member wanted to help make the vision come true. Six years later, Total Transit was taking 16,000 calls a day, had the largest fleet of Prius vehicles in the country, and was dispatching a fleet of over 1,200 cabs. Revenues now exceeded $180 million—and the company created six millionaires.

Attract, Hire, and Coach Winners

Total Transit's leadership never loses sight of the fact that the company is a service company, so that, ultimately, it all comes down to the moment when the employee and the customer come in contact. At that moment, winners must represent Total Transit, which starts with the hiring process.

The company uses assessments and evaluations to determine as much as possible about candidates. Candidates who are selected for an interview face a series of one-on-one interviews in addition to a group, or panel, interview. The team uses the technique of integrity interviewing to surface each candidate's trustworthiness and integrity. One new hire joked that he had to come in for seven interviews before he received an offer.

Chief executive Mike Pinckard underscores the importance of the selection process at Total Transit, saying, "I'd rather have a gap go unfilled, no matter how hard that is, than hire the wrong person. I learned in my time as a baseball player in college and the minor leagues that to improve a team, the next person added has to be better than the average of all the existing players."

Getting the right people can even influence the choice of a company's location. When the team launched the technology company, Veyo, they decided to headquarter it in San Diego, in the heart of the local tech environment, to ensure the ability to attract, hire, and retain the very best people.

The company's ability to attract, hire, and coach winners is clearly proved by the awards and accolades it and its team have received in recent years. Two years in a row, the company was named the best place to work in metropolitan Phoenix. The company's CFO, Larry Eisel, was named CFO of the Year. A driver for Discount Cab, Al Tracy, was recognized in 2015 as Taxicab Driver of the Year by the Taxicab, Limousine & Paratransit Association. Total Transit was named a Top Corporate Giver, Top 10 Family-Owned Company, and a Fastest-Growing Company over multiple years by the *Phoenix Business Journal*.

Build an Autonomous Company

At one point, Hughes sold Discount Cab Company, but he was forced to take the company back when the buyer went through personal bankruptcy. Hughes successfully rebuilt the business, but growth eventually stalled at $10 million.

Hughes realized that although his tight hold on the reins had allowed the company to survive, it was also choking growth. So he brought in new, highly qualified talent and learned to delegate to the appropriate level in the company. The new team took up the challenge, and growth exploded.

To maintain an autonomous company, Total Transit invests in the ongoing development of its leaders. Several operating unit presidents and senior managers are members of Vistage executive peer groups and regularly attend monthly meetings with other executives to challenge their thinking and resolve issues.

Mike Pinckard also participated in Harvard University's Owner/President Management Program (OPM), a forty-year-old program that helps executives and entrepreneurs around the world reach their leadership potential.

The company's rigorous hiring process achieves the first step in building an autonomous company by bringing in the right people. Delegation and decision-making are moved to the point closest to the client or customer, reflecting the management team's trust in employees' abilities to make decisions and, more importantly, to learn from their mistakes. Pinckard points out that this is sometimes harder in the short term but works well over the longer term because it reduces the cost of supervision and ensures that senior managers are focused on moving the company to the next level rather than day-to-day decisions.

Celebrate Successes

Total Transit holds regular meetings to celebrate the birthdays and anniversaries of team members, and Hughes sends handwritten notes home which contain movie tickets and restaurant gift cards.

To encourage employees to recognize each other, the company built a website called The Total Transit Way. There, employees can praise one another and give verbal high-fives for a job well done. Senior management also encourages employees to offer feedback and test new ideas via the website.

The company founded The Total Transit Foundation, a 501 (c)(3) nonprofit, to serve internal and community initiatives. The foundation's incentives and programs to encourage employees to give back to the community include:

- **Employee-of-the-Month donation**—Each month, the foundation's leadership selects an employee of the month who exemplifies the company's core principles and donates $500 to the employee's favorite charity.
- **Matching-gift program**—The foundation's matching-gift program, designed to encourage employees to support

US-based nonprofit organizations, offers a way for employees to combine their personal contributions with foundation gifts for greater impact. All full-time employees are eligible to participate in the program.

- **Scholarship program**—The foundation's scholarship program assists the children and grandchildren of Total Transit employees and driver-contractors who want to further their education. Scholarships up to $10,000 are awarded based on academic achievement, demonstrated leadership potential, and financial need.

To help the disadvantaged in the community help themselves, the foundation supports many charitable community organizations and campaigns throughout the year by providing transportation services or financial support. Organizations that the foundation has partnered with include Free Ride Back, Tumbleweed Youth Center, Habitat for Humanity, Pink Ride, St. Mary's Food Bank Alliance, Homeward Bound, Save the Family, and Emerge Center for Domestic Abuse.

Chapter Seven

Celebrate Successes

The CEO Tools Business System

COMMUNICATE • EXECUTE • OPTIMIZE

The more you praise and celebrate in life,
the more there is in life to celebrate.

—Oprah Winfrey

Jack hopped off his new bike after a fifteen-mile practice ride and locked it near the water station and the bench. Slipping on his running shoes, he immediately began his mental preparations for the three miles he'd now run.

Jack was training for his first triathlon—a Sprint Triathlon, which included a quarter-mile swim, a thirteen-mile bike ride, and a 5K run. He was following his training plan religiously and tracking his progress against his personal metrics.

When he completed his run, he spotted his mentor, seated on the bench and clapping quietly.

"Nice bike!" his friend said. "You're really stepping things up."

"Yeah," Jack replied. "I'm training for a triathlon, so I've added cycling to my routine." He talked about his training plan and the metrics he was tracking.

"Looks like what you're doing to improve your business is spilling over into other areas of your life," the man said.

Jack shifted the discussion to the conversations they'd just had at work about the point person for each key area of the business. "I was pleased— and surprised—to find that people are excited and proud to own a piece of our performance."

"That's great," his mentor said. Then came the now-standard question: "Do you mind if I ask you a couple of questions?"

"I'd be disappointed if you didn't," Jack answered.

"My guess is that people are now pushing pretty hard, working more hours, and that they really care about the results they're getting, right?"

Jack nodded proudly.

"How do you celebrate that work, those results, and that dedication? What are you doing to encourage and even compensate people to make sure that effort continues?"

"I haven't really thought about that," Jack admitted. They'd made progress, but most of the goals were a quarter or more away from being achieved. And it would be months before they held annual performance reviews, when raises and bonuses were discussed.

"That's what happened when I led Courtesy Coffee Company in San Diego," his mentor said. Jack was amazed at how much experience this man had amassed in so many companies.

"I was a first-time chief executive, and our goal was to grow sales from $1.2 million to $2.5 million in two years. The bad news was that

we didn't make it. The good news was that we grew to a little over $2 million, a 67 percent jump.

"Our big mistake was that we didn't appreciate what we had accomplished. We felt like we'd missed the target, and we didn't celebrate at all. As a result," he said, "morale plummeted.

"Then I came across Jack Stack's book, The Great Game of Business. *Stack stresses how important it is to have metrics and to assign individual responsibilities, and he emphasizes the need to create many ways to win and celebrate—not to hinge everything on a single make-or-break outcome."*

He continued. "I applied those lessons at GAC Printing. We set big, audacious goals, monthly and quarterly. We achieved our quarterly BAGs in sixteen quarters in a row. Sometimes we missed our monthly goals, but by stretching toward them, we achieved so much more in the end. So, we thought, why not celebrate the improved results—even though, technically, we'd failed? We celebrated that we'd given it our all, which kept the effort in high gear, even when we were falling short.

"Celebrating doesn't have to mean a trip for the team to Las Vegas or Cabo San Lucas," he added. "Celebrating success is more of an attitude, a philosophy. Create a culture where you notice when people do things right, and make recognition and celebration a natural part of the company culture."

He took out his trusty pad and wrote down eight ways to recognize and celebrate:

CREATE CELEBRATION AND ACCOMPLISHMENT

1.	Compensation	2.	Recognition
3.	Fun	4.	Personal Growth
5.	Challenges	6.	Convenience
7.	Communication	8.	Security

"Thanks," Jack said. "This feels like the perfect way to continue our momentum. And our people deserve it. They've worked hard and produced great results. I'm proud of them, and I want them to know it," Jack said with a feeling of intent.

"By the way," Jack continued. "I feel a little silly asking you this after all the time we've spent together . . . but . . . what's your name?"

His mentor burst into genial laughter, stood up, and started walking away.

"Who are you?" Jack called after his friend.

The man, still chuckling, called back over his shoulder, "Just call me Kraig."

Have you ever wondered why some of your goals for your company remain just out of reach? Setting the direction and establishing meaningful goals gets your people headed in the right direction; but what makes the quest personally meaningful and tangible for the *individual employee* is to offer a reward or celebration once the goal is achieved.

Companies that take time to celebrate and recognize people achieve far more than those that don't. They create an ongoing, self-perpetuating cycle of celebration and recognition that leads to greater and repeated results—which in turn leads to further celebration and recognition. Celebration becomes the *fuel* that drives the growth engine.

Equally important, when you celebrate achievement, you confirm that your goals are important enough to be recognized. If you don't celebrate successes, the goals lose their meaning and significance. And achievements can even become counterproductive in the absence of celebration.

Remember Courtesy Coffee Company in San Diego? The company set a goal to grow from the flat $1.2 million, year-after-year revenue to $2.5 million in two years. The company missed that mark but still grew revenue to $2 million. Sadly, they focused on missing the goal—and didn't celebrate the admirable results they *had* accomplished.

What could the coffee company have done differently after falling just shy of its goal? It could have done these two things:

- **Recognize the team effort**—Look for what went well and recognize those accomplishments. Acknowledging the victories, no matter how small, helps set up the new goals for the following year.

- **Recognize the high contributors**—Even when the bull's-eye is missed, there's always someone who's done exceptional work and is deserving of special recognition. By recognizing your people and clearly communicating your appreciation, you show them that their efforts were worthwhile—even when the team misses the mark. People will contribute more going forward and work even harder toward the next goal if their previous contributions were recognized and valued.

The truth is, people want more than a paycheck. Sure, money's important. But your employees also want challenging work with opportunities to learn and grow. More importantly, they want to know that their hard work is contributing to a positive outcome. That's why celebrating success is so important. It shows that everyone from the top of the company down to their peers appreciates their hard work and recognizes their personal contribution to the results.

> The Gallup organization found that the No. 1 reason most Americans leave their jobs is that they don't feel appreciated. Before you think this wouldn't happen at your company, consider that 65 percent of people surveyed said they got no recognition for good work last year. None. Nada. At your next team meeting, look to your right and then to your left, and consider that the odds show that one of those two people doesn't feel appreciated for his or her contribution.

Celebrate the Milestones

Too many companies approach celebration as all or nothing. They wait until they achieve the year-end numbers or reach the big, audacious goal before breaking out the balloons and banners. If you wait to reach the finish line before you acknowledge and reward the efforts of your people, you'll lose a lot of employee energy along the way.

Think of running an Ironman triathlon. It's the ultimate physical challenge, as well as a mental, even spiritual, endeavor. The competitors who finish have prepared themselves mentally, tracked their progress, and rewarded and reassured themselves along the way, throughout the hours of swimming, biking, and running. They focus on the celebration that comes at the end, which creates a continuing aspiration to win. They picture themselves crossing the finish line. This is what keeps the athlete going despite a grueling pace.

It's important to celebrate the milestones along the journey to success. And it's our job as managers and leaders to cheerlead, thank, and praise our employees for their good performance all along the way.

Marathons are another test of mental and physical endurance. Over the 26.2-mile course, people cheer on the runners, hand out water, and hold up banners and signs to celebrate the competitors' progress. In San Diego, California, at the Rock 'n' Roll Marathon, they even have bands along the route to spur on and energize the runners.

When you break down big goals into smaller achievements, you make the goals both easier to accomplish and easier to recognize along the way. You can apply many of the tools discussed in earlier chapters—such as the monthly letter, walking the four corners (W4C), and personal notes sent home—to recognize these milestones and the employees who were instrumental in getting you get there.

A remarkable and impressive best-selling book by Gary Markle, *Catalytic Coaching: The End of the Performance Review*, reinforces this concept. Markle outlines a way to coach employees to improve their performance without the hated, much-maligned annual review. He discourages readers from celebrating or criticizing performance only at the end, which he says is not effective because it comes across as judgment. Continuous coaching that includes repetitive communication and repetitive recognition, by contrast, has the greatest impact on performance and results.

Start with a Self-Assessment

So how do you start celebrating in your company? Do you suddenly need be the funny, happy, life-of-the-party type? Not at all—unless you want to be. You do, however, need to find a few people who are naturally gifted with a sense of fun and enthusiasm. Then, you need to support them as they add a spirit of genuine joy and celebration to your organization. Of course, your own authentic enthusiasm is needed to communicate to the troops that celebration is an important part of the company culture.

A simple self-assessment is a good place to start. By self-scoring your company, department, or group, you'll discover areas that need a tune-up.

This model is based on the CEO Tools 8-Score, which is often used to measure employee satisfaction. Each of eight key criteria that people want from their jobs is scored on a scale of one to ten by both the company leader and individual team members.

The 8-Score	CEO	Team Mbr 1	Team Mbr 2	Team Mbr 3	Team Mbr 4	Team Mbr 5	Average
Compensation	8	6	8	6	7	7	7.0
Recognition	7	7	6	5	6	6	6.2
Fun	6	5	6	5	5	6	5.5
Personal Growth	7	5	7	5	6	6	6.0
Challenge	8	6	7	5	6	7	6.5
Convenience	5	5	5	4	4	5	4.7
Communication	7	6	6	4	6	6	5.8
Security	8	7	7	5	7	6	6.7
Averages	7.0	5.9	6.5	4.9	5.9	6.1	6.0

In the above example, we see a company that challenges and compensates employees fairly well, although not generously. The company isn't considered a fun place to work nor is it seen as providing conveniences to its people. The scores, which average an unimpressive 6.0 overall, show that improvements are possible in all eight areas.

Note that the CEO is a little more optimistic about the company's programs than the employees—which isn't unusual. It would be a great time for this leader to use the W4C tool to tune in to what employees are thinking and ways to boost these employee ratings.

Tools for Celebration

Chances are, your company could use some improvements in at least some of these eight areas. Here are some tools in each area that you can incorporate to motivate your employees and reward them for their efforts.

Compensation

Whenever new goals are set, compensation must be aligned with those goals. Nothing is more demotivating than working hard to achieve a big corporate goal without a financial reward. Compensation must be a part of the plan. Too often, companies set new goals but forget to align the comp plan.

Your payouts to employees must be timely and tied to the results. In companies that pay annual bonuses, employees and managers can forget the reason for a year-end bonus. Incentives should be paid at the time of performance—or monthly or quarterly.

> Raphael Crawford-Marks, chief exec of Bonusly, a rewards and recognition company, notes in *Fast Company*: "Let's say an employee stays late every night one week in April to save a major project. As a manager, you want to recognize his efforts, so maybe you thank him and make a note of that for when the time comes for year-end bonuses. The problem is, by December, that project might be a vague memory for the employee, and while he might be happy to receive a hearty check, the significance in reward for the specific event is lost.

This may not mean you should move *completely* away from annual bonuses. It simply encourages you to rethink how your total recognition budget is allocated and to consider how you can use all elements of compensation, recognition, and rewards most effectively to make a real impact on your culture.

Annual bonuses, in fact, work best for senior executives, based on their annual achievement toward three-year or five-year goals and objectives. This prevents sacrificing the future for short-term results and focuses the team on the big picture. All other employees, however, will benefit from a monthly or quarterly incentive program.

Recognition

Survey data routinely show that leaders aren't good at providing appropriate recognition to their employees. Yet nothing has more impact on great performance than recognition—and the payoff is much higher than for compensation alone.

When done well, recognition is part of a strategic program that includes awards, acknowledgments, kudos, and fun. It usually takes a team of people who are naturally gifted in the area to accomplish it most effectively.

> If you're wondering how much to invest in a recognition program, consider allocating 1 percent of the payroll. A study by SHRM/Globoforce showed that 85 percent of companies that spent 1 percent or more of payroll on recognition saw a positive change in employee engagement. Anything under this amount doesn't get significant results, and amounts above this showed somewhat diminishing returns.
>
> And that's not all. Companies with strategic recognition programs reported employee turnover rates almost 25 percent lower than those without a program. Happier employees equals lower turnover. What more do you need?

You may be thinking that you pay your people well, and that's enough. Don't be fooled. A good compensation system does not substitute for recognition. Compensation and recognition address different human needs.

Remember college psychology 101 and Maslow's hierarchy of human needs? Chip Conley, founder of JDV Hotels, adapted Maslow's famous pyramid for his business. His hierarchy for employees shows that compensation meets a base need or expectation. In other words, people expect to be paid fairly for the work they do and the results they achieve. Recognition begins to meet the second-level need of self-esteem and self-worth; it's not expected—it's appreciated. It's personal and important, and it's what people remember and share with others. When you fill this need, your people won't quit and go work somewhere else just because they were offered more pay.

If you want to create a "sticky" retention structure, the third and highest level of Conley's employee pyramid is to give people something they didn't even *know* they wanted: allow them to feel part of something bigger than themselves.

Some companies find ways to make giving back part of their fundamental business model. Tom's Shoes donates millions of pairs of shoes to the less fortunate around the world. Patagonia, the outdoor clothing company, donates 1 percent of profits to benefit the outdoors areas that their customers frequent and love.

Other companies create such tight corporate cultures that people can't imagine leaving because it would upset their whole social structure. FedEx and Zappos.com are two examples. Employees of these companies, which resonate with a fraternal feel, become close friends with each other.

Still others use ownership to accomplish the feeling of being part of something bigger than oneself. Companies with an employee stock ownership program (ESOP), like Jack Stack's companies in Springfield, Missouri, come to mind. In this structure, the company is owned by the employees, who have a vested interest in the company's success.

Never overestimate the importance of giving recognition to get results or, if you prefer, praise for performance. To get repeated results, recognition must be consistent. It's an ongoing cycle of perform → praise → perform → praise → perform.

Just ask anyone who has received a Bravo Zulu award at FedEx. FedEx's Fred Smith borrowed the concept from his military days in Vietnam. Bravo Zulu, or BZ, is a naval signal, typically conveyed by a flag hoist or over voice radio. It means "well done" with regard to actions, operations, or performance. FedEx has pins and plaques with the Bravo Zulu symbol and stickers that managers can add to letters and notes to recognize employee performance. It may sound a little like the gold stars you got on your homework when you were a child, but it works and it's motivating.

Every manager at FedEx is authorized to give out a $100 cash award or a certificate for a dinner, concert, or other event. FedEx managers together award over 20,000 BZs each year, and the company spends an estimated $2 million annually on this recognition program.

Fun

Having fun is what sets great companies apart from all the rest because fun keeps great people there who enjoy getting results. Unfortunately, most companies don't have much fun.

To make fun an integral part of your company culture, consider appointing a CFUNO (chief fun officer). Masters of fun in business are Michael Houlihan and Bonnie Harvey, founders of Barefoot Wine, the best-selling wine brand in the United States. Among their creations are Barefoot Days and Free Wine Fridays.

Barefoot Days are paid days off in months without a US holiday when businesses are typically closed: March, April, June, August, and October. Imagine the power of reminding your people that Monday will be a day off for *Your Company* day. Do you think your people would brag to friends and family about their upcoming three-day weekend due to *Your Company* day? Of course they would!

On Free Wine Fridays, every Barefoot Wine employee is handed a bottle of wine by one of the owners, who says, "Thank you for your efforts," and tells the employee to enjoy the weekend on Barefoot. Of course, it doesn't hurt that the company is in the wine business, but that isn't why they do it. They do it because it's *fun*.

At Zappos.com, it's not unusual to see a parade winding its way through a department, orchestrated by *another* department to say thanks for a job well done. Neither is it unusual to find Tony Hsieh or the other founders and executives serving meals at the employee cafeteria to show their appreciate for and mingle with employees. The company even encourages employees to recognize *each other*, empowering every employee to give a co-worker $50 for going above and beyond.

How about giving each of your executive team members a $50 or $100 bill each month to award to an employee they caught doing a good job? Tell them the money must be distributed by the end of the month, and that they have to report what happened when they gave it away at the next executive team meeting. Imagine the positive buzz that you'll create at your company!

> To know what to recognize and celebrate, use the tracking tools from chapter three to track recognition. Remember WGMGD (*What Gets Measured Gets Done*)! Tracking recognition works. The definition of having fun always includes true performance, growth, and profits. Make performance, growth, and profits a precursor to your celebrations.

Make it fun to be a part of your company, and your people will spread the word—and that enhances your employer brand.

Personal Growth

Opportunities for personal and professional growth play a key role in attracting and retaining good people. One way to foster personal growth is to give your employees good business and self-help books. Pick out the books you want them to read and write a personal note on the title page. You can use business best-seller lists as a source of good reading material—or better yet, give out copies of a book you're currently reading.

Top-performing companies have extensive training and/or learning programs. At Zappos.com, for example, employees can check out a book from the company's extensive lending library of business books.

Challenge

People thrive on challenges. Mihaly Csikszentmihalyi, author of *Flow: The Secret to Happiness,* defines the ideal work environment as one where the current work is enough of a challenge that it's just outside the current skill set of the person or team doing it. That's to say, the work requires a stretch, and the stretch is where all growth occurs.

When people don't have challenging work, they die on the job—or at least "retire" while still on the job. They may keep showing up; however, they slow down and do less work while continuing to collect a paycheck.

One of the best ways to maintain a highly engaged workforce is to create ongoing challenges for yourself and your employees. Do this by developing big, audacious goals (BAGs) together, and use quarterly priorities managers (QPMs) or quarterly business reviews (QBRs) to reinforce the importance of these objectives and to acknowledge performance.

> Companies with strong cultures are often built around a big challenge. Sam Walton once said, "High expectations are the key to everything."

Convenience

One way to keep employees happy is to create more personal time for them. You're probably saying, "Are you crazy? I need them to work more, not less!" The fact is that most will work harder for you if you can give them more time for themselves when they aren't at work.

Your employees probably spend a fair amount of time on weekends running errands and checking things off their personal to-do lists. What if you could give them back several hours each weekend by making common routine tasks available to them at work? It's not hard to do.

Contract with a local dry cleaner for dry-cleaning pick-up and delivery; bring in a manicure team once a week; order from a meal preparation service and have it delivered to the office; or offer a car-wash service once a week through a mobile wash company. This is how your employees, using no more than their break time, can save themselves hours of coveted weekend time.

You can also give employees more personal time by shortening their home-to-work commute—and it's easy to do. Broaden your core business hours to extend from 7 o'clock in the morning to 6 o'clock in the evening, and let your employees decide on the eight-hour period they want to work. Flex time, which is very popular in the business world today, not only shortens employees' commutes by allowing them to travel during nonpeak periods, it also communicates that you trust them to put in the required thirty-five or forty hours a week—when it works best for them and their families.

Communication

This topic was covered extensively in chapter two, and this is a reminder of its importance. As noted in that chapter, in survey after survey, employees who are asked, "What do you want more of?" say they'd like more communication and recognition for their contributions.

Security

People need to feel secure in their jobs—physically secure in their persons, intellectually secure with the application of their ideas, mentally secure in being open and honest, and spiritually secure in their personal beliefs. How are you providing for these needs?

Here are some things you can do to help your people feel more secure:

- Recognize your employees, and their sense of job security will increase.

- Provide for employees' physical safety in and around the facilities, including the parking lot.

- Build a company culture of trust that includes a culture of listening respectfully.

- Give employees credit when you use their ideas, to enhance their intellectual safety.

- Create a business values statement that is lived out each day, to foster employees' spiritual security.

Do you wonder how security ties into celebration? One definition of celebration is "happiness practiced as frequently as possible." How can people be happy if they don't feel secure?

Security is at the base of Maslow's hierarchy of needs, and people can't rise to higher levels of happiness and self-esteem unless their basic security needs are met. They'll perform at much higher levels when their basic needs are no longer distractions.

Peer Recognition Programs

There's no reason for recognition to come only from the top. In the best-performing companies, recognition goes up, down, and sideways. Peer recognition programs—which give all employees the power to elevate their peers by acknowledging great performance—are one of the best tools for creating a culture of celebration.

> A study by the Society for Human Resource Management and Globoforce showed that peer-to-peer recognition is almost 36 percent more likely to have a positive impact on financial results than manager-only recognition programs.

Peer recognition motivates people to do what best-selling author Ken Blanchard was famous for teaching: "Go out there and catch someone doing something right!" You may need to fan the flames at first to encourage people to engage, but the flames will quickly become a wildfire of positive praise.

CTSI in Memphis developed a peer recognition program called STAR Awards under the leadership of Ken Hazen. Employees issue certificates to one another to acknowledge a job well done or a positive contribution made to a project. The certificates are redeemable for company-logoed items and gifts from a catalog. Visiting the CTSI offices, it's not uncommon to see the cubicles and offices of their highly engaged employees wallpapered with STAR Awards.

Another idea is to use recognition Buck$ as a fun way to allow employees to reward each other. In this approach, employees each receive a certain number of Buck$ forms at the start of every year that they are free to award to co-workers. The Buck$ can be converted to logoed items or merchandise. You can give employees Buck$ forms and challenge them to catch people doing things right for either a customer or another employee.

Zappos.com has a Zollar Program that's a lot like Buck$. Employees can rack up points on a gift card and then buy items like gym bags, water bottles, and desk fans.

Peer recognition programs offer you a chance to have fun and be creative—so pull out all stops. One company imprints an image of the top executive's face on its Buck$ award. And another encourages employees to draw a little face or scene in the center of a Buck$ award, which looks like a dollar bill.

Here are some tips for developing a peer recognition program at your company:

- **Award information**—Be sure that there's a place on your awards for three things: the name of the award presenter, the name of the award recipient, and the reason the award was given.

- **Award reason**—Coach employees to be specific about why they are giving a co-worker an award. "Sara went out of her way to serve the customer" is good, but coach employees to be more specific: "Sara spent hours helping Susan Rockrise from Esprit® solve a critical production problem." Being specific informs employees what they've done to warrant an award and reinforces the behavior you'd like to see repeated.

- **Role for HR**—Have HR track the giving and receiving of all awards and prepare a quarterly report.

- **Top giver reward**—Every quarter, reward the employee who gave the most awards. Hold a public recognition ceremony and make it a very big deal.

- **Top recipient reward**—Present the top award recipient with an all-expense-paid weekend with a spouse, significant other, or friend to a special getaway or a generous gift certificate for shopping or to an upscale restaurant. Be sure to change this reward on a regular basis to keep it fresh and exciting. When you award *experiences*, you make the award live on in the recipient's memory.

There are numerous companies that you can engage to administer your award programs, or you can manage them in-house. In either event, be sure to create programs that have a *social aspect* and are tied to a system of points that convert to company-logoed items or catalog items. And double-down on the recognition by having a public display of the awards or a leaderboard in a public area for all to see.

Executive Recognition Programs

One of the ultimate tools for the development of leaders is membership in an executive peer group such as Vistage, Renaissance Executive Forums, Chief Executive Network, Convene, TAB, EO, and YPO. These organizations conduct monthly meetings that are limited to peers at the executive level and include diverse industries and business models. The members present and discuss the major challenges and opportunities their businesses face and receive valuable input from the other members. Many of the programs include an executive coaching component.

The power of receiving objective, unbiased feedback from executive peers—whose only agenda is to help each other build a company that runs more effectively and to encourage each other to live more stress-free lives—is without equal.

One of the ultimate tools to use for senior leaders and managers is an investment in their ongoing development. This could include management development and training programs at universities or through training companies like Crestcom or Sandler Sales.

Recognition Ads and Posters

Some companies run ads in newspapers, business journals, or trade publications to celebrate a company success and honor their employees. Such ads not only recognize your employees, but also send a positive message about your company to employee prospects, your customers, and the community at large. By including an employee photo in the ad, the impact is even greater.

Another way to create visibility for employees whose contributions you want to recognize is to create your own posters and display them prominently throughout your building. Saint Joseph's Hospital of Atlanta and Team Industries, Inc. near Milwaukee both use this technique. They hang the posters after business hours so the award recipients will be surprised when they arrive the next morning.

The same approach works to recognize your customers and suppliers. Put up posters in your offices, plant, and warehouse that recognize your customers' and suppliers' employees who are especially helpful to work with.

These posters are a great way to welcome new employees as well. Imagine the anxiety of their first day turning to excitement and enthusiasm when they see a poster with their picture welcoming them to their new job. It will help others recognize them as well.

Of course, these posters can be electronic if your company places display screens around the facility to offer information and recognition.

Personal Notes to Thank and to Recognize

As leaders, we have an obligation to write thank-you notes to our people. It's important to thank the people who make us successful, particularly when today's pace often keeps us from expressing thanks when we should.

There's a slight difference between thank-you notes and recognition notes. The idea is to thank for an effort and to recognize for results.

In today's highly competitive employment market, where it's hard to find and keep good people, few things have greater impact on employee morale and engender more company loyalty than a sincere thank-you note from a boss or supervisor that's mailed to the employee's home.

Here are some tips on writing an effective note:

- **Start the note with *you*, not *I***—To underscore the employee's contribution, use *you* and *your*: "*You did an excellent job at . . .*" "*You demonstrated your unique skills in . . .*" "*Your contribution to the XYZ project was invaluable . . .*" Avoid using *I*, as in: "*I appreciate what you did . . .*" "*I want to thank you . . .*"

- **Provide specifics**—State what the employee did and the effect the employee's actions had on the project, goal, etc. The formula is action/effect, action/effect: "*When you gave up your holiday weekend to work on the XYZ project, we were able to deliver the product by the due date and reach our goal of on-time order fulfillment.*"

If you skip over management levels when doing this, always check in with the employee's supervisor first, who may have some current information that you should consider in writing the note.

Writing personal notes doesn't take much time, but it does take some discipline to write them regularly. Consider setting a day and time every two weeks to write your notes. Whatever you must do to ensure that your employees receive a timely personal note of recognition from you, do it. When it comes to your employees' morale and dedication, a personal note from you is very hard to beat.

Focus on Winners

Successful business people get the best results when they focus their efforts on what yields the biggest return on their time, energy, and money. One of the key leverage points in any company is to support winners—the people who produce the best results day after day, month after month, year after year—and to spend time with them.

Winners in your organization aren't hard to identify. They're your salespeople with the top sales rankings. They're the production managers whose lines have the best metrics year after year. They're accounts receivable clerks who consistently have the lowest days sales outstanding. Or they're the new account reps who bring in the most and highest-margin accounts. These are the people who, no matter what the task or challenge, get it done and done well.

The No. 1 rule for recognizing winners is that you can't do too much of it. Be sure that your superstars know how much you appreciate their good work. Send meaningful messages that recognize these top performers to everyone else in the company. For example, write individual notes to your winners on a regular basis to remind them how well they're doing and how much you appreciate their extra efforts—and especially their consistent results. At the same time, send a monthly message to the entire team to recognize these top performers—the team members who consistently beat their own performance records.

It should go without saying that you should always pit people against their own prior performance, not against co-workers. And of course, you should never publicly call out underperformers. Handled properly, your underperformers will work to raise their performance so that they, too, will be acknowledged.

> Your messages should be, as author Mickey Connolly once described, "a call to greatness, not a cause for embarrassment."

You might be tempted to help those who struggle. But if you spend an hour a week with a $10 million-a-year salesperson rather than a $1 million-a-year salesperson—and increase the performance of both by 20 percent—which yields the bigger return on your time investment?

So instead of devoting time to help an underperforming employee, send the employee a short note of encouragement: "You've had a tough go of it for the past month or two, but we have every confidence that you'll attain your goals. Let your supervisor know what he can do to support you and help you get there."

The greatest gift you can give your people is your time and attention. Help your employees become winners and stay winners by giving them more of your time and attention, but do it proportionately:

a bit more time for winners, a good amount for top performers, and somewhat less for all others.

Awards, Awards, Awards

Most companies give out annual awards like Top Salesperson of the Year or Circle of Excellence, and the like. But why reward only the top one or two people in your company only once a year? What if you recognized as many of your employees as winners as often as possible?

• • •

GAC became famous for making a big deal of a highly sought-after Quarterly Sales Award, which was presented to all salespeople who hit their numbers for the quarter. There was also a celebration for Sales Region of the Quarter from the company's seven regions. Each quarter, the executives personally thanked the winners and presented them with a memento, such as a logoed cap or other item of apparel, or a specially minted logoed silver dollar.

Imagine the company executives wheeling clothing racks through the 386,000-square-foot headquarters and fitting logoed jackets on every employee on all three shifts.

• • •

This kind of over-the-top recognition helps create the Power of *WE*. It also creates indelible memories for you and your team.

Top Tools to Celebrate Successes

- **Awards, awards, awards**—Create a program of monthly, quarterly, and annual awards. You can't overdo employee recognition. If you're not comfortable giving awards, appoint someone else who is. Celebration is vital to the success of an organization.

- **Regular celebrations**—Report against key goals and regularly celebrate the ones you achieve. Your people will respond with repeated superior performance.

- **Personal notes home**—Send personal, handwritten thank-you and/or recognition notes to your employees' homes to encourage repetition of their efforts.

- **Peer recognition programs**—To extend recognition, have employees recognize each other for positive actions. As Ken Blanchard said, "Go out and catch someone doing something right."

- **Grand solution**—Offer something employees really want or need but can't or won't purchase for themselves in recognition of their role in achieving a key goal.

- **Walk the four corners**—Recognize and celebrate daily successes by walking around your building to talk with people. Go out every day to say "thank you" to an employee.

Top Tools to Become a Better Recognizer

- **Positive feedback**—Pat people on the back as they make headway on a job or at its conclusion. Examples: "It's great to see your progress on that project." "Looks like you'll set a new sales record this year." "Thanks for the hard work. And congratulations on winning that bid!"

- **Cheerleading**—Talk up the achievements of the company—daily. Examples: "Our productivity sure is picking up lately." "Did you hear the news about our profit growth?"

- **Listening**—Listen to people's problems. Example: "Would you share that with me?"

- **Encouragement**—Encourage and compliment people whenever possible. Example: "You should try your good idea about . . ."

- **Resources**—Find ways of being helpful to your team members. Example: "I saw this article that may tie into what you're working on."

- **Positivity**—Generate hope; there's always light at the end of the tunnel. Example: "This storm will pass; they all do. We'll be better for the struggle."

- **Mediating**—Get people to feel better, no matter how the interaction started. Example: "What can we do to make this work out better for everyone involved?"

For Further Reflection

- Are you having fun? How can you add more fun to your work?
- Are you making sure your team is enjoying working at your company?
- Do you measure employee satisfaction and take action to keep it high?
- Do you track and measure the number of fun events and their impact on employees on an ongoing basis?
- Do peers have a way to thank and recognize each other for a job well done?

CEO Tools Case Study:
Barefoot Wine, Santa Rosa, California

Most people would be amazed to hear that the largest wine brand in the world began as a start-up in the laundry room of a rented farmhouse in the Sonoma County hills. But that's where Michael Houlihan and Bonnie Harvey started this venture—with no money and no real knowledge or experience in the wine industry. Fast-forward ten years later, and Barefoot Wine had become an enduring success, selling over 600,000 cases per year. By the time Houlihan and Harvey sold the brand to E&J Gallo in 2005, they'd won a ton of awards and helped transform an entire industry from stuffy and intimidating to fun, casual, and socially aware.

How did the two end up in the wine business? A mutual friend who was a grape grower in Sonoma County, Mark Lyon, had delivered his product to a winery that subsequently faced financial difficulty. Houlihan was a consultant at the time, and he offered to help negotiate the terms of Lyon's payment. After some wrangling, it was agreed that Lyon would take ownership of the wine that had been produced but not bottled. Houlihan and Harvey then worked a deal to use the wine producer's production line to bottle the wine and then take the product to market so Lyon could be paid. For Houlihan and Harvey, this meant creating a brand, labels, and a distribution network to sell the wine.

Houlihan and Harvey half-seriously described it as their get-rich-slowly scheme. Along the way, they not only recouped Lyon's funds but also built Barefoot Wine into an iconic brand in the huge and complex global wine industry.

Their effort paid off—and it has continued to pay off. Barefoot Wine was named a "Hot Brand" in 2016 for the fourteenth year in a row by *Impact* magazine, one of the wine industry's leading trade publications. To be considered for this award, brands must maintain at least 15 percent year-over-year growth.

Set the Direction

Barefoot Wine was built on the spirit of an entrepreneurial culture. The two founders defined their culture as:

- **Serving a bigger cause**—This involved developing strategic allies and creating "worthy-cause" marketing.
- **Customer-focused and sales-driven**—They built a culture that was customer-centric and customer-responsive, which was driven by their sales team.
- **Right people and high engagement**—They worked to have the right people who were properly incentivized with the appropriate controls and permissions in place.
- **Right compensation, recognition, and appreciation**—The energy of the company was fueled by recognition and appreciation.
- **Balance of information, accountability, and permission**—The culture was built on sharing the needed information, accountability to action, and permission to make mistakes.
- **Fun**—They encouraged making business fun and getting to know the individuals on the team.

Houlihan and Harvey had a very unique way of defining their vision for the company. They wanted a vision that every employee could see and understand. The vision they created and reinforced was:

Everything at Barefoot Wine comes from the customer: jobs, position, money, and resources.

The mission of Barefoot Wine was succinct: Making the best wine at the best price. The product has more than lived up to the superlative "best," because Barefoot Wine is the most awarded wine brand in the United States to date, boasting over 2,500 awards.

Communicate to Build Trust

The key to building trust is to listen. Because they lacked experience in the wine business, the two founders listened to everyone. They framed questions to anyone who touched the product, from clerks to buyers, and from distributors to forklift drivers—and they received real, actionable answers. Store buyers and grocery clerks told them what wine sizes and packings were needed in the market. The bottling line manager shared his experience on which labels worked and which ones didn't—and why. A forklift operator suggested they use color-specific cartons for different products to reduce delivery errors. They implemented all these suggestions.

Track Metrics and Give Feedback

To stay ahead in a very competitive industry, Barefoot Wine relied on a dashboard of metrics. A key report in the dashboard was the Cliff Report. Like the Cash Report in *CEO Tools 2.0*, the report analyzed cash, receivables, and borrowing capacity versus expenses and payables. Houlihan and Harvey dubbed this the Cliff Report because it told them how long they had before they went over the cliff!

They analyzed profit per varietal and used the bottle report to track each cost component of a bottle of wine: the cork, the label, the glass, the foil, and any taxes. This allowed them to track individual costs of production year-over-year rather than just cost of goods sold.

They took an interesting approach to determine the cost of sales. In this metric, they analyzed every element involved in making a sale, including taxes in a specific geographic area, product returns, customer service costs, transportation and travel costs to the market, discounts needed to secure sales, samples provided, marketing and advertising costs, and promotions. Barefoot Wine created this distinction for cost of sales to keep it from being lumped into an overhead number like selling, general, and administrative. They wanted to indicate that these were costs that they could impact and control, not unallocated overhead.

Anticipate and Create the Future

The two founders believed in making their mistakes work for them, which meant having conversations about about everything that could go wrong or did go wrong. They called these conversations "awfulizing sessions." The point was not to lay blame or upset or embarrass anyone. Quite the contrary, these sessions were designed to figure how to address and correct things that had gone sideways.

One such session was used if they'd made a mistake, founded on one of their favorite sayings: Never waste a good mistake. Without blame or judgment, they discussed ways to address the issue to be sure it didn't happen again. The responsibility of the person experiencing the mistake was to work with the team to fully document the process so that the entire team could benefit from the learning.

Another type of session was called "Get Smart About Stupid." The idea was to anticipate any potentially stupid, careless, or even reckless things that could happen if someone slipped up or was not paying full attention. Then they designed a way to avoid the mistake and fully documented the process to ensure that it never occurred.

Get, Coach, and Keep Winners

Barefoot Wine's first rule for getting the right people in place was to hire for culture, not to get a job done. Their criterion was simple: look for the things that can't be taught. For Barefoot, this was distilled down to two things: integrity and hustle.

They defined *integrity* as taking personal responsibility for behavior and having a nonblame orientation. To determine integrity, they asked candidates about their biggest mistake.

The key was whether the candidate took full responsibility for the mistake or blamed others.

Barefoot Wine defined *hustle* as a sense of urgency, of being in motion, of having movement, and keeping busy. To identify hustle, they closely observed each candidate during the interview:

- How did they sit?
- How did they enter and exit the room?
- Did they take notes and ask questions?
- They asked candidates if they'd ever developed metrics for performing well at a job or position. They invited candidates to take a walk with them and noted the following:
- How did they move?
- Did they look ahead, scanning, or stare down at their feet?
- Could they walk and talk at the same time comfortably?

Barefoot Wine used all this information to determine the level of hustle a person would bring to the job.

On the last day of interviews, they did something very unique: they did *all* the talking. They reviewed a summary of the compensation package and what the company did, how they did it, and the challenges the business faced. They discussed how the job fit into the big picture and how it supported the sales function. Then they asked the candidate to write a one-page summary of what they'd heard. The candidate was told to include what was said, how they would fit in, and what they could contribute. The assignment was to be submitted by 5:00 p.m. the following day.

Many candidates didn't complete the assignment. Those who did helped the hiring team determine the best person for the job since the candidate had explained how they would contribute and the value they would bring.

Build an Autonomous Organization

To create an autonomous company, Houlihan and Harvey built what they called a "know-the-need" culture in direct contrast to the "need-to-know" approach that other companies take.

In a need-to-know culture, employees feel isolated, aren't respected for their creativity and intelligence, and are seen as part of the problem. And solutions come from a few, top-down.

In Barefoot Wine's culture, people feel part of a team, are respected for their creativity and intelligence, and are seen as part of the solution. Solutions come from many, bottom-up.

The steps to build a need-to-know culture are simple: share problems and challenges with everyone, and involve everyone in the solutions.

Barefoot Wine created a culture that gave employees permission to take risks and make mistakes. This approach empowered people to take risks and try new things, but it also held them accountable for making the process better to avoid recurrences of problems. The phrase that captured this was, "Don't blame, take aim." The key wasn't to simply fix the problem; it was to provide a long-term systemic solution to prevent it from happening again.

Celebrate Successes

Barefoot Wine built a culture that relieved pressure and encouraged creativity, and a big part of the culture was having a certain irreverence for convention. Their employees were encouraged to customize their work experience to keep *it* interesting and *them* engaged.

They were allowed to write their own job descriptions—with their managers' approval. In fact, no one was allowed to keep the same job description for more than one year. And they could choose their own job titles. Michael Houlihan had the title "head stomper." Bonnie Harvey was "the first foot," and CFO Doug McCorkle became "the cork."

Another unusual part of working at Barefoot Wine was their annual five-card draw for jobs. In this activity, employees could discard parts of their jobs they didn't like, and others could pick them up. In turn, they would pick up the job parts that other people had discarded. Asked what would happen if a job task was discarded and no one picked it up, Michael Houlihan said, "It never happened, because we selected people who were go-getters. Someone was always looking to prove themselves by taking on new responsibilities."

Since they hired for hustle, there was a culture of wanting to do more and be recognized to get ahead. Employees also knew that they'd only have to do it for a year, and if they didn't like it, they could discard it the next time around.

Barefoot Wine celebrated and rewarded employees in these and other ways:

- Birthdays off with pay
- Health club memberships
- Staff lunches
- Reserved parking spaces at work
- Wine for the weekend

Epilogue

Jack was enjoying his run this morning. His pace was brisk, but he wasn't pushing himself too hard. He took time to notice the trees and the lake, then watched as a hawk soared and cried out overhead. A deer stood at the ready, just off the trail. Sensing no threat, she never moved as Jack ran by. Their eyes met for a brief moment.

Jack had never noticed all this before. When he'd started running, he was busy thinking—actually, worrying—about his company. Later, he was consumed with trying to make it better. Then, he was focused on driving to achieve something bigger.

Now, Jack was enjoying the journey. The company was in capable hands and producing strong, profitable results. Jack could be there and be engaged—or not—as the situation required.

As he crested the hill and marveled at the spectacularly colored clouds from the sunrise, he was a bit saddened to see that the bench was empty. He slowed to a walk and approached the bench that had been the seat of so many important lessons that had changed his company, his team, and himself.

As he got closer, he noticed that, while his companion was not seated in his usual spot, something was there in his place. It was a book. Jack picked it up and read the words on the cover: CEO Tools *by Kraig Kramers. A handwritten note accompanied the book.*

Dear Jack,

I'm so pleased the lessons you have learned and tools you have applied have produced such great results for you. I have moved on to help another CEO in need. I think you now have everything you need to make your company all you had hoped it could be. Keep celebrating your successes.

By the way, congratulations on the triathlon. I was there when you crossed the finish line.

All the Best,
Kraig

Jack thought about the progress that he and his management team had made when they put into practice what he'd learned from his friend and mentor. He was scheduled to start the annual planning process later in the month and was excited about what the future held for the company. Holding the book in both hands, Jack looked up at the sky and said, "Thanks, Kraig. Thanks for everything."

About the Authors

Kraig Kramers was the author of *CEO Tools: The Nuts-n-Bolts of Business for Every Manager's Success*. Published in 2002, the book became the go-to manual for CEOs who wanted to build strong, profitable companies that would last into the future.

When Kraig died in 2014, Aprio, LLP in Atlanta, Georgia, purchased the CEO Tools assets and decided to update and revise the original version of the book.

Jim Canfield is proud to have been selected to pick up where Kraig left off by authoring this new version of Kraig's book, continuing to build and improve the tools, and working directly with companies interested in implementing this powerful system.

CEO Tools is now powered by Aprio, LLP, a leading CPA-led advisory firm with a distinguished partner group headed by a visionary CEO, Richard Kopelman.

Made in the USA
Columbia, SC
20 March 2021